DARK HORSES
JUMPS GUIDE 2021/22

Marten Julian

Published in 2021 by Marten Julian
69 Highgate, Kendal, Cumbria LA9 4ED
Tel: 01539 741 007
Email: rebecca@martenjulian.com

Copyright © Marten Julian 2021

The rights of authors Marten Julian, Jodie Standing & Ronan Groome to be identified as the authors of this work have been asserted in accordance with the Copyright, Designs and Patents Act 1988.

All rights reserved. No part of this publication may be reproduced, stored in a retrieval system, or transmitted in any form or by any means, electronic, mechanical, photocopying, recording, or otherwise, without the prior written permission of the publishers.

A catalogue record for this book is available from the British Library.

ISBN: 978-1-8380647-9-2
ISSN: 2633-4267

Cover design by Steve Dixon
Designed by Steve Dixon

Photography: Francesca Altoft (unless stated) & Susan Parker
Cover photograph: Francesca Altoft

CONTENTS

INTRODUCTION	5
THE PREMIER LIST	6
THE DARK HORSES	18
JODIE STANDING'S TEN TO FOLLOW	34
THE IRISH CONTINGENT	49
THE BUMPERS	60
THE CHAMPION HURDLE PREVIEW	76
THE GOLD CUP PREVIEW	93
INDEX	116

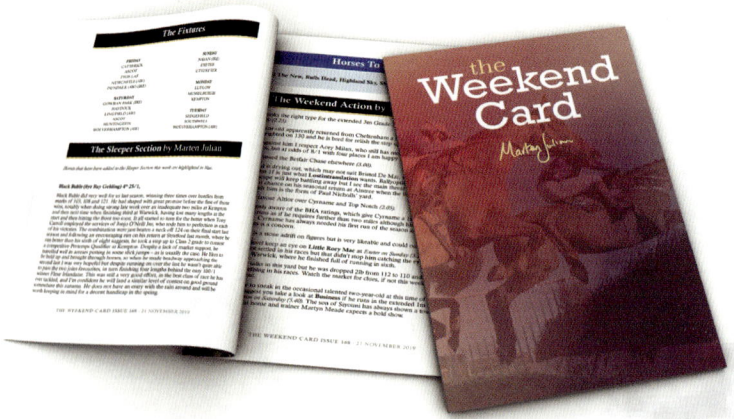

CONTINUITY IS THE KEY TO SUCCESS!

THE WEEKEND CARD

About: Our Weekend Card includes weekly racing news from Marten Julian, Ian Carnaby and Jodie Standing with regular guest contributors. After 40+ years experience one thing that has become clear is the importance of continuity in a service. For example, when we select a horse we know that our clients would appreciate some feedback – whether it wins or loses. The Weekend Card prioritises this by providing weekly updates on key horses from Marten's Dark Horses Annuals (both Flat and Jumps), as well as selected horses from earlier editions of the Weekend Card.

Info: Clients can pick whether to receive it through the post, via email or online. Available to download from a Wednesday evening. For postal subscribers we post it First Class every Thursday.

Phone Line for postal clients: No need to miss out on selections. Free access to Weekend Card selection line for clients without email or internet. The line is on an 03 phone number which means all calls are normal landline charges – we pay the additional charge for you!

Worth noting: Past copies available to view online or we can post out upon request.

Contact us for a free information pack.

Telephone: 01539 741 007 / **Email:** rebecca@martenjulian.com

www.martenjulian.com

Write to: FREEPOST MARTEN JULIAN
(nothing else required on the envelope)

WEEKLY RACING INFORMATION!
Packed with over 5000 words of thought-provoking content!

INTRODUCTION

Hi there!

Thank you for buying this 2021/22 edition of the *Dark Horses Jumps Guide*. I hope that you find it a useful source of reference and enjoyment throughout the course of the season.

As always I have had the support of a talented team to assist me with the content, production and marketing. Without their support this book would not have been possible.

I am greatly indebted to Jodie Standing for her research and contributions and also to my daughter Rebecca and Steve Dixon for their help at the production stage. Ronan Groome is thanked for his feature on the Irish challenge and, as always, Ian Greensill has done a sterling job with the proofreading.

I want to make a special mention also to Francesca Altoft for providing such wonderful images.

If you wish to keep updated with my latest news and the running plans and progress of the Premier List qualifiers then they can be monitored in the *Weekend Card*.

You can also hear my views and news on a daily basis on 0906 150 1555, where any selections are given in the first minute of the message (calls charged at £1.50 a minute at all times).

If you would prefer an alternative means of acquiring this information, without paying premium rate charges, then please call Rebecca (01539 741007) for details of the *Telephone & Text Service*.

Finally I would like to wish you all the very best of good fortune in the months to come.

Bye for now.

The Premier List
Marten Julian

The following horses are selected in the belief that they possess the attributes to have collectively made a profit to level stakes by the end of the season.

BASS ROCK (5YO BAY GELDING)

TRAINER:	SANDY THOMSON
PEDIGREE:	MARTALINE – HORTA (ASSESSOR)
FORM:	5/22321 -
OPTIMUM TRIP:	2M 4F +
GROUND:	SOFT

Has the profile of the type of horse his shrewd owner likes to earmark for a decent race.

Showed ability on his sole start in France as a three-year-old in July 2019 when fifth of 13 over hurdles before appearing for these connections in a novices' hurdle at Carlisle last October, staying on well to finish second. Filled the same spot over the course and distance the following month.

Stepped up to an extended 2m 4f in heavy ground at Ayr in January, finishing third of nine, and subsequently had wind surgery.

Reappeared at Ayr in March and ran second in a match before making a successful handicap debut at the same track in April, comfortably beating Leostar with more in hand than the margin reflects.

Now rated on 123, he looks nicely poised to win a chase or two around the northern and Scottish circuits.

DUSART (6YO BAY GELDING)

TRAINER: Nicky Henderson
PEDIGREE: Flemensfirth – Dusty Too (Terimon)
FORM: 13 -
OPTIMUM TRIP: 2m +
GROUND: Good/Soft

Extremely promising half-brother to high-class performer Simonsig and other useful types.

Made a successful hurdling debut at Newbury in November 2020 when beating the subsequently useful Soaring Glory with something in hand, with the talented Amarillo Sky back in fourth.

Jumped the hurdles with air to spare and subsequently had time off until reappearing at Aintree in April in the Grade 1 Betway Top Novices' Hurdle.

Tracked the leaders and led briefly two hurdles from home before a clumsy jump cost him momentum. Stayed on again on the run to the line to finish third, beaten two and a half lengths by County Handicap Hurdle winner Belfast Banter.

Jumped his hurdles in the manner of a chaser and expected to take high rank in that sphere this season. Has the pace to win over two miles but the pedigree to excel over further.

Dusart – a potential top-class novice chaser

EDWARDSTONE (7YO BAY GELDING)

TRAINER:	ALAN KING
PEDIGREE:	KAYF TARA – NOTHINGTOLOOSE (LUSO)
FORM:	222/1126/5U1353 -
OPTIMUM TRIP:	2M 4F +
GROUND:	GOOD/SOFT

Consistent and relatively lightly raced seven-year-old who can resume his career over fences.

Has always shown ability – second in three bumper races in 2018/19 – and ran notably well when chasing home the useful Chantry House at Warwick in March 2019.

Switched to hurdling the following November, made an immediate impact when winning a novice event at Wincanton and then when beating Harry Senior by a length in a better race at Aintree.

Not disgraced next time out, when second in a Grade 2 novice contest at Haydock, before running on well to finish sixth of 15 to Shishkin in the Supreme Novices' Hurdle at Cheltenham in March.

Returned to action last November in the competitive Greatwood Handicap Hurdle at Cheltenham, catching the eye with a strong-finishing fifth to The Shunter.

Unseated his rider on his chase debut at Doncaster in December and quickly returned to hurdling the following month when winning in heavy ground at Market Rasen from a mark of 141.

Ran the best race of his career when third, beaten four and a half lengths, in the prestigious Betfair Hurdle at Newbury.

Again shaped well when fifth of 25 to Belfast Banter in the County Hurdle at Cheltenham before ending the season with a good third in the Grade 3 Pertemps Network Handicap Hurdle at Aintree in April. Ended the season on a mark of 150 and is now expected to resume his chasing career.

Bred to stay three miles but has the pace to win at shorter trips. Has shown his form on all types of ground and is confidently expected to prove one of the season's top novice chasers.

Has the option of returning to hurdles if required.

FAKIERA (6YO BAY/BROWN GELDING)

TRAINER: Gordon Elliott
PEDIGREE: Cokoriko – Stella D'Engilbert (Network)
FORM: 4/4222/11240 -
OPTIMUM TRIP: 2m 4f +
GROUND: Soft

French-bred six-year-old with the stamina to excel over a distance of ground.

Has proved a consistent performer over his three seasons, only twice finishing out of the first two from 10 starts.

Ran fourth of 22 on his bumper debut at Fairyhouse in April 2019 and then fourth again on his return to action in a Leopardstown bumper in December.

Finished runner-up on his next three starts over hurdles, shaping well on each occasion but proving one-paced at the finish.

Won his first race on his seasonal return last November, keeping on strongly to beat Gabynako by a nose in a 2m maiden hurdle at Fairyhouse.

Stepped up to 2m 4f later that month to win the Grade 3 Monksfield Novice Hurdle at Navan by half a length before returning to the track just under a month later to finish second over the same distance.

Raised in class to a Grade 1 2m 6f novice hurdle at Leopardstown in February, equipped with sheepskins for the first time, plugged on in gritty fashion to finish fourth behind the useful Gaillard Du Mesnil.

Went to post well fancied for the 3m Albert Bartlett Novices' Hurdle at Cheltenham, expected to appreciate the longer trip, and appeared to have every chance when moving smoothly two hurdles from home only to weaken quickly before the last and finish 33 lengths behind the winner.

Has an awkward way of galloping and carries his head quite high. Short of speed but is an immensely likeable individual blessed with great tenacity.

Has the profile and potential to become a useful staying chaser.

FIVE O'CLOCK (6YO BAY GELDING)

TRAINER: Willie Mullins
PEDIGREE: Cokoriko – Rodika (Kapgarde)
FORM: 0/32/2110/
OPTIMUM TRIP: 2m 4f +
GROUND: Soft

Half-brother to French Grade 3 winner Highway To Hell and chase winner Irish Dance out of an unraced half-sister to a Listed winner over hurdles.

Shaped well in three starts in France in 2018, showing progressive form over hurdles, soundly beaten on his debut in April 2018 before showing a turn of foot to finish third just over one month later.

Displayed tenacity on his next outing in June, putting in some sloppy jumps before almost being brought down at the flight before the turn for home. Recovered the ground quickly and again showed a turn of foot approaching the last, failing by just a short neck to win.

Joined this yard later that year and made his debut for these connections in a 2m 5f hurdle at Tramore in December 2019. Finished second at short odds but won his next two starts at Limerick in January and then over 2m 5f at Thurles a month later.

Final outing of the season came off 145 in the Martin Pipe Conditional Jockeys' Handicap Hurdle at Cheltenham, losing his position as the pace quickened leaving the back straight before recovering the ground on the final turn. Taken wide and still many lengths behind the leader approaching the final flight, he then stayed on very strongly to finish seventh – beaten four and three-quarter lengths.

Missed last season but reported back to full fitness and either has the option of exploiting his mark over hurdles or embarking on a campaign over fences.

Acts on heavy ground and bred to stay three miles.

GERRI COLOMBE (5YO BAY GELDING)

TRAINER:	Gordon Elliott
PEDIGREE:	Saddler Maker – Ruse De Guerre (Cadoudal)
FORM:	1/11 -
OPTIMUM TRIP:	2m
GROUND:	Soft

Just one of a handful of young novice hurdle prospects in his powerful yard, with the potential to prove the best of the bunch.

Was all out to win a modest point-to-point at Lingstown in March 2020 and bought for £240,000 shortly afterwards at Cheltenham. Made his debut under Rules for these connections in January, effortlessly winning a bumper at Fairyhouse in the heavy ground by 24 lengths.

Reappeared just over a month later at Naas and beat Walter Grey by three and three-quarter lengths, with subsequent winner Forged In Fire five lengths further back in third.

Half-brother to a 1m 6f winner in France out of a well-related daughter of Cadoudal.

Very well regarded by his trainer and should take high rank in his new discipline.

HOLLOW GAMES (5YO BAY GELDING)

TRAINER: Gordon Elliott
PEDIGREE: Beat Hollow – I'm Grand (Raise A Grand)
FORM: 1/11 -
OPTIMUM TRIP: 2m +
GROUND: Soft

Very exciting son of Beat Hollow who was bought for £255,000 soon after winning a point-to-point at Turtulla in March 2020.

Made his debut for these connections in a bumper at Punchestown in November, cajoled along half a mile from home before taking the lead and quickening instantly to beat subsequent winners The Banger Doyle and Sin A Bhfuil, eased down towards the finish.

Again displayed a turn of foot to win what turned out to be a high-class bumper at Leopardstown in December, beating subsequent dual winner Eurotiep and bumper winner Lispendense with something in hand.

Closely related to 2m 5f hurdle winner Moyode Gold out of a half-sister to the smart Tumbling Dice from the family of top-class performer Remittance Man.

Already displaying a high level of form and will take top rank as a hurdler, possibly over further than two miles.

Has shown a significant turn of foot.

MIGHTY POTTER (4YO BAY GELDING)

TRAINER: Gordon Elliott
PEDIGREE: Martaline – Matnie (Laveron)
FORM: 1 -
OPTIMUM TRIP: 2m +
GROUND: Soft

Hard to assess from the evidence of his only run last season, but displayed a sparkling turn of foot to win a Punchestown bumper in March and should prove a useful recruit to hurdling.

Half-brother to point-to-point and 2m 4f hurdle winner French Dynamite and 2m hurdle winner Indiana Jones out of a successful dual-purpose family.

The form of his race did not hold up to inspection but there was no mistaking the ease in which he won and he looks another potential top novice hurdler for his powerful yard.

MISTER COFFEY (6YO BAY GELDING)

TRAINER: Nicky Henderson
PEDIGREE: Authorized – Mamitador (Anabaa)
FORM: 1/12/1304
OPTIMUM TRIP: 2m 4f
GROUND: Soft

Likeable half-brother to useful dual-purpose performers in France from the family of Group 1 winner Bint Pasha.

Has consistently finished strongly in his races over hurdles, suggesting he should improve when stepped up to three miles.

Won on his bumper debut for Harry Whittington at Huntingdon in April 2019 before changing hands for £340,000 at Doncaster the following month.

Made a highly satisfactory debut over hurdles that December, beating useful performers Shakem Up'Arry and On To Victory, before running second at Huntingdon a month later. Returned last season with a success from a mark of 128 at Sandown, quickening impressively from the second last in the manner of a good horse to win by five lengths.

Kept on to finish third over the same course and distance in December before again doing strong late work when seventh in the Betfair Hurdle at Newbury.

Ran a similar race stepped up to 2m 4f at Aintree in April finishing fourth of 22.

Will need to settle better in his races if he is to realise his potential but has already displayed a decent level of form and looks like developing into a useful novice chaser.

Very consistent and blessed with a turn of foot.

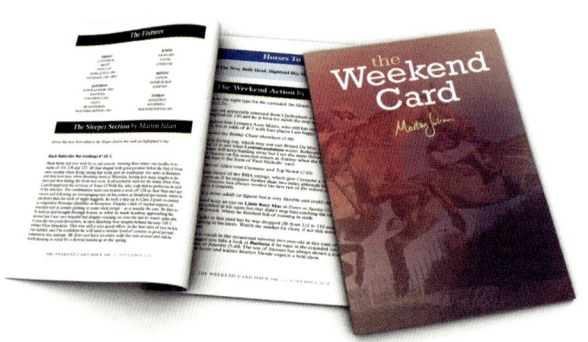

LATEST NEWS ON HORSES FEATURED IN THIS PUBLICATION

WEEKLY RACING INFORMATION!
Packed with over 5000 words of thought-provoking content!

RED LION LAD (5YO BAY GELDING)

TRAINER:	David Pipe
PEDIGREE:	Flemensfirth – Hotline (Poliglote)
FORM:	1/363 -
OPTIMUM TRIP:	2m 4f +
GROUND:	Soft

Intriguing son of Flemensfirth who appears to have been campaigned with handicap chases in mind.

Beat subsequent bumper winner Thunder Rock by 10 lengths in a point-to-point at Ballyarthur in March 2020, and subsequently bought privately by these connections in July.

Has hinted at better things to come in three starts over hurdles, despite not being the most fluent of jumpers, when third on his debut at Exeter in December then sixth of 12 at Ffos Las in February, before catching the eye when staying on again into third over an extended 2m 3f at Chepstow three weeks later.

Dam's family traces back to high-class chaser Master Minded.

Rated 115 over hurdles and could be placed to win from that mark, but his future is probably over fences.

Has been given a wind operation during the summer and likely to prove an effective performer when stamina is at a premium.

The Dark Horses
Marten Julian

The following horses, mostly unexposed, have shaped with sufficient promise to suggest they will progress to better things.

BROOMFIELD BURG (5YO BROWN GELDING)

TRAINER:	Nicky Henderson
PEDIGREE:	Sageburg – Somedaysomehow (Old Vic)
FORM:	10 - 11
OPTIMUM TRIP:	2m 4f
GROUND:	Soft

Third foal of a hurdle-winning daughter of Old Vic from the family of top staying chasers Maid Of Money and Ten Of Spades.

Won a point-to-point from two subsequent winners in October 2020 and was then bought for £90,000 by these connections.

Reappeared last January in a Newbury bumper, well supported in the market but forfeited all chance when refusing to settle. Showed his true form in his next two starts, winning at Southwell in May in a canter and then with similar ease on his hurdling debut later that month at Warwick.

Looks the type of horse who could be placed to win a competitive handicap hurdle before embarking on a career over fences next season.

Has untapped potential and is worth monitoring closely.

CROSSING THE BAR (4YO BAY GELDING)

TRAINER: Philip Hobbs
PEDIGREE: Poet's Voice – Ship's Biscuit (Tiger Hill)
FORM: 0/0 - 2144
OPTIMUM TRIP: 2m +
GROUND: Good

Interesting recruit to hurdles, having left the impression he had unfinished business for Sir Michael Stoute on the Flat.

Acquired for 60,000gns in September by this trainer having won a 1m 6f 0-80 handicap at Carlisle in May but beaten in next two starts.

Half-brother to useful stayers Mekong, Pow Wow and Cochise out of a well-related half-sister to Group 2 winner Hi Calypso.

Comes from a very successful family, with the potential to progress to better things both on the Flat and over hurdles.

DRAGONFRUIT (6YO CHESTNUT GELDING)

TRAINER: Oliver Greenall
PEDIGREE: Black Sam Bellamy – Fruity Farm (Weld)
FORM: 2P/404516P0 -
OPTIMUM TRIP: 3m
GROUND: Soft/Heavy

Not as exposed as his form figures suggest, having shaped well over hurdles before making a successful chase debut from a mark of 105 at Carlisle in December.

Only sixth of 13 nine days later at Huntingdon over hurdles and never going well next time at Chepstow back over fences. He then jumped poorly when finishing well beaten at Newcastle in March.

Half-brother to the useful 3 m 2f hunter chase and point-to-point winner Fruit Fayre and other fair performers from a very successful family.

Looks the type who could win a marathon test at a modest level in the mud at a long price.

Interesting.

EL BARRA (7YO BROWN GELDING)

TRAINER: WILLIE MULLINS
PEDIGREE: RACINGER – OASAKA (ROBIN DES CHAMPS)
FORM: 2/10421 - 1
OPTIMUM TRIP: 2M +
GROUND: SOFT

Expected to prove a useful recruit to fences provided he remains sound.

Bought for £280,000 in May 2018, shortly after running second to the now-rated 153 Fury Road in a useful point-to-point at Dromahane.

Easily won a bumper on his first outing for these connections at Thurles last November but then finished down the field after breaking a blood vessel on his hurdling debut at Leopardstown in December. Again disappointed when beaten on his next two starts but ended the season on a happier note with victories in April at Fairyhouse and Punchestown.

Has not been without his problems but should win plenty of races over fences provided his troubles are behind him.

FRENCHY DU LARGE (6YO GREY GELDING)

TRAINER: V<small>ENETIA</small> W<small>ILLIAMS</small>
PEDIGREE: A<small>L</small> N<small>AMIX</small> – Q<small>UADENCE</small> D<small>E</small> S<small>IVOLA</small> (M<small>ANSONNIEN</small>)
FORM: 22/23/42361 -
OPTIMUM TRIP: 2<small>M</small> 4<small>F</small> +
GROUND: S<small>OFT</small>

Not as exposed as his placings suggest, despite having finished in the first three in seven of his nine starts.

Showed ability in bumpers, running second three times and third once from four starts in 2019/20. Returned last season over hurdles, showing up well in his first four outings before winning over 2m 5f in heavy ground at Ludlow from a mark of 111.

Raised 9lbs to 120, could win again over hurdles but is more likely to be switched to fences.

Just the type of horse his trainer excels with and is one to note over a distance of ground when the mud is flying.

GRANGECLARE WEST (5YO BAY GELDING)

TRAINER: Willie Mullins
PEDIGREE: Presenting – Hayabusa (Sir Harry Lewis)
FORM: 1 - 1
OPTIMUM TRIP: 2m +
GROUND: Soft

Acquired for £430,000 in December 2020, shortly after winning a point-to-point at Lingstown by four lengths. Half-brother to two chase winners out of a half-sister to the useful 3m 2f winner Gunner Welburn.

Started a very short price to make a successful debut under Rules in a bumper at Punchestown in May and duly delivered, showing a fine turn of foot to beat subsequent winners Salvador Ziggy and Watergrange Jack with plenty in hand.

Expected to prove one of the best recruits to hurdles this season and bred to be effective over further than two miles.

HILLCREST (6YO BROWN GELDING)

TRAINER: Henry Daly
PEDIGREE: Stowaway – Shop Dj (Dushyantor)
FORM: 21 -
OPTIMUM TRIP: 2m 4f +
GROUND: Soft

Put up a truly remarkable display when winning a bumper at Wetherby in March, under strong pressure and looking held five lengths off the leader until staying on dourly to get up in the final strides.

Had failed by just a nose to make a winning debut at Doncaster in January, again needing plenty of cajoling half a mile from home.

Half-brother to 2m 4f hurdle winner Bold Record out of a well-related winning daughter of Dushyantor.

Unlikely to come into his own until tackling fences and a distance of ground, but has shown exceptional tenacity in his two races to date and looks the sort of horse who could pop up at a decent price when the emphasis is on stamina.

JONBON (5YO BAY GELDING)

TRAINER:	NICKY HENDERSON
PEDIGREE:	WALK IN THE PARK – STAR FACE (SAINT DES SAINTS)
FORM:	11 -
OPTIMUM TRIP:	2M
GROUND:	SOFT

Full brother to top-class performer Douvan from a useful French family.

Won his sole point-to-point at Dromahane by 15 lengths in November 2020 and was subsequently bought for £570,000 at Goffs UK later that month.

Travelled well before making a successful Rules debut in a bumper at Newbury in March, shaken up before pulling clear to beat Flying Demon by four and a quarter lengths.

Justifiably enjoys a tall reputation and has shown enough to suggest he may live up to the family name.

KINCARDINE (4YO BAY GELDING)

TRAINER:	Nicky Henderson
PEDIGREE:	Kayf Tara – Side Step (Norse Dancer)
FORM:	1
OPTIMUM TRIP:	2m 4f +
GROUND:	Soft

Stoutly bred half-brother to 2m 5f hurdle winner Steal A March out of a bumper-winning half-sister to 2m 7f winner No Trumps, tracing back to the family of Spanish Steps.

Won a Southwell bumper in May, keeping on well despite having to be switched two furlongs from home.

Did well to win over two miles around a sharp track given the stamina in his pedigree.

Should prove effective in novice hurdle company, probably over a distance of ground.

MASACCIO (4YO GREY GELDING)

TRAINER:	Alan King
PEDIGREE:	Mastercraftsman – Ange Bleu (Alleged)
FORM:	12 -
OPTIMUM TRIP:	2m
GROUND:	Good/Soft

Could prove an exciting recruit to hurdles for his talented trainer following two promising displays in bumpers last season.

Kept on strongly to win a 1m 5f Junior National Hunt Flat Race at Doncaster in November, beating subsequent winner Arthur's Seat cosily at the line.

Returned from a lengthy break at Ayr in April and was unlucky not to win again, making strong late headway from a poor early position to finish full of running half a length behind the winner.

Comes from a very successful family, a half-brother to seven Flat winners including US Grade 1 winner Angara and other performers at a high level. The dam is a half-sister to Breeders' Cup winner Arcangues.

Has the pedigree to win on the Flat and may have a touch of class over hurdles.

MERCUTIO ROCK (5YO BAY GELDING)

TRAINER: JONJO O'NEILL
PEDIGREE: MARESCA SORRENTO – MONDOVI (LINDA'S LAD)
FORM: 424 -
OPTIMUM TRIP: 2M 4F
GROUND: SOFT

First foal of a winning hurdler and closely related to high-class chaser Saint Calvados.

Has shown promise in three runs, fourth on his debut in a Chepstow bumper last October and then second on his hurdling debut at the same track four weeks later, despite jumping poorly in the latter stages of the race.

One-paced when fourth of 12 at Uttoxeter in December and ended his season on a mark of 112.

Should be capable of winning a handicap hurdle, probably over a longer trip, but his future is over fences.

Acts well in the mud and sure to be placed to optimum effect by his canny handler.

MR GLASS (5YO BAY GELDING)

TRAINER: Paul Nicholls
PEDIGREE: Sholokhov – Maryota (Martaline)
FORM: 311 -
OPTIMUM TRIP: 2m +
GROUND: Soft

Full brother to 2m 5f hurdle winner Sunrise Ruby and half-brother to 2m 4f hurdle winner Skin Deep out of a half-sister to high-class but not always reliable Yanworth.

Ran third on his debut last November in a Newbury bumper – form held up very well – before keeping on strongly in the heavy ground to win a bumper at Wetherby in December by 11 lengths. Made all under a penalty to beat two rivals at Haydock in March.

Has always schooled well at home and has the potential to prove a classy recruit to hurdles. Does not lack speed but should stay beyond two miles.

MULBERRY HILL (5YO BROWN MARE)

TRAINER: Fergal O'Brien
PEDIGREE: Califet – Massini Rose (Dr Massini)
FORM: 0P0F2 - 2212
OPTIMUM TRIP: 2m 6f +
GROUND: Good/Soft

Talented mare who has shaped well in her early starts this autumn and has the potential to progress later in the season.

Was beaten in six runs in Irish point-to-points but shaped well in her final two starts, running second at Fairyhouse in April and then runner-up again at Lisronagh a fortnight later.

Joined these connections shortly afterwards and shaped with great promise on her hurdling debut at Worcester in July, staying on strongly in the closing stages from arrears to finish second to high-class dual-purpose prospect Heartbreaker.

Confirmed that promise over the same course in August, again held up in the early stages before leading at the second last and pulling clear to win going away by nine and a half lengths from the 102-rated Present Storm.

May not have been suited to the track when dropped back in trip next time at Market Rasen, finishing second to hurdling debutant Haseefah.

Half-sister to a point-to-point winner from the family of 2m 6f chase winner Inistioge.

Has done well to show such useful form at this stage of her career and could prove a useful staying mare in better company next spring.

Mulberry Hill – an exciting prospect for the spring (Susan Parker)

MURVAGH BEACH (6YO CHESTNUT GELDING)

TRAINER: Nicky Richards
PEDIGREE: Doyen – Magic Park (Carroll House)
FORM: 6/5602 -
OPTIMUM TRIP: 2m 4f +
GROUND: Soft/Heavy

Interesting prospect from the family of Gold Cup winner Kicking King and other useful performers.

Beaten a long way on his sole start in a bumper in March 2020 but shaped with more promise than his finishing position suggests in his first three starts over hurdles, beaten a total of 119 lengths. Particularly caught the eye on the second of those starts when plugging on steadily up the hill, to finish with running left, in a 2m 1f hurdle on heavy ground at Carlisle in November.

Ran from a mark of 93 on his handicap debut at Newcastle in March over an extended 2m 4f, quietly supported in the market and always prominent until getting outpaced turning for home. Found a second wind and rallied approaching the second last to take second place towards the finish, beaten one and three-quarter lengths by the winner.

Raised 5lbs from 93 to 98 and looks a ready-made winner of a handicap hurdle over three miles, with the potential to develop into a useful staying chaser.

Appears to be favourably handicapped and acts well in the mud.

O'TOOLE (5YO CHESTNUT GELDING)

TRAINER:	STUART CRAWFORD
PEDIGREE:	MAHLER – ON GALLEY HEAD (ZAFFARAN)
FORM:	1 - 2
OPTIMUM TRIP:	2M 4F +
GROUND:	SOFT

Promising son of Mahler and bred to stay, being a half-brother to 2m 7f hurdle winner Pride Of Pemberley. Dam, a bumper winner and a half-sister to useful performer Dare Me.

Stayed on dourly to win by 15 lengths on his debut in a Fairyhouse bumper in February and then second, again sticking on very gamely, to high-class performer Kilcruit in a top-class contest at Punchestown two months later, finishing ahead of Cheltenham Champion Bumper winner Sir Gerhard back in third.

Reported to have schooled well at home and confidently expected to prove a useful prospect over hurdles, especially when stepped up in trip.

Very gutsy.

ROYAL ARCADE (6YO BAY/BROWN GELDING)

TRAINER: Nicky Richards
PEDIGREE: Arcadio – Miss Excitable (Montelimar)
FORM: 213 -
OPTIMUM TRIP: 2m +
GROUND: Soft

Promising half-brother to 4m hunter chase winner Excitable Island out of an unraced half-sister to useful performers Emma Jane and Captain Americo.

Shaped with promise in three runs at Carlisle, finishing second on his hurdling debut on heavy ground in February and then winning very easily over the same course and distance four weeks later.

Dropped away tamely when third of six later that month at a time when the yard's horses were not right.

May be capable of winning over hurdles from a mark of 122 but his future lies in novice chases.

Showed a touch of class when on song and could be the type to build up a sequence on the northern circuit.

SUPREME GIFT (4YO BAY GELDING)

TRAINER: HENRY DALY
PEDIGREE: GETAWAY – PRAIRIE CALL (OSCAR)
FORM: 4 - 1
OPTIMUM TRIP: 2M 6F +
GROUND: SOFT/HEAVY

Just the sort to do well for this most patient of handlers.

Looked an out-and-out stayer when fourth on his point-to-point debut in April 2021, but improved on that opening effort when winning at Tattersalls Farm the following month.

Third foal of a hurdle-winning half-sister to 2m 3f winner Lights Of Broadway from the family of Gold Cup winner Imperial Call.

Unlikely to be the quickest horse in training but will come into his own when tackling a distance of ground, with the promise of further improvement when he switches to fences.

THREE STRIPE LIFE (5YO BROWN GELDING)

TRAINER: GORDON ELLIOTT
PEDIGREE: LEADING LIGHT – HIRAYNA (DOYOUN)
FORM: 14 -
OPTIMUM TRIP: 2M +
GROUND: SOFT

Promising son of Leading Light, a half-brother to three winners over 2m 4f up to three miles.

Displayed an impressive turn of foot when winning a Navan bumper by nine lengths in January, beating subsequent winners Outlaw Peter, now with Paul Nicholls, and Now Where Or When, a winner of a maiden hurdle at Fairyhouse in April.

Next appearance came in the prestigious Weatherbys Champion Bumper at Cheltenham, on edge at the start and running keen, but shaping well in third a furlong from home until dropping back to fourth towards the finish.

Rated one of the leading bumper performers last season and confidently expected to transfer that ability to hurdles.

VINA ARDANZA (4YO BAY GELDING)

TRAINER: Gordon Elliott
PEDIGREE: Califet – Go Noble (Golan)
FORM: 1 -
OPTIMUM TRIP: 2m 4f
GROUND: Good/Soft

Travelled with a lot of class when beating the promising Masaccio by half a length on his sole start in a bumper at Ayr last April.

May have been fortunate to beat the second but has subsequently joined a top yard and expected to make a big impression over hurdles.

Half-brother to 2m 3f hurdle winner Botani out of an unraced half-sister to useful staying performers.

Did well to show such pace given his stout pedigree and promises to become a useful performer over timber.

ZINC WHITE (3YO GREY GELDING)

TRAINER:	OLIVER GREENALL
PEDIGREE:	VADAMOS – CHINESE WHITE (DALAKHANI)
FORM:	566 - 11
OPTIMUM TRIP:	2M
GROUND:	GOOD/SOFT

Cost £310,000 at the June Sales and a half-brother to useful performers The Trader, Misty Grey and Chinese Jade out of a Group 1-winning daughter of Dalakhani.

Unraced over hurdles but won both his starts on the Flat for former trainer Ralph Beckett, over 1m 6f at Wetherby and over the same trip at Sandown in May.

Rated 87 on the Flat, handled soft ground well and expected to prove a useful recruit to hurdling for his new connections.

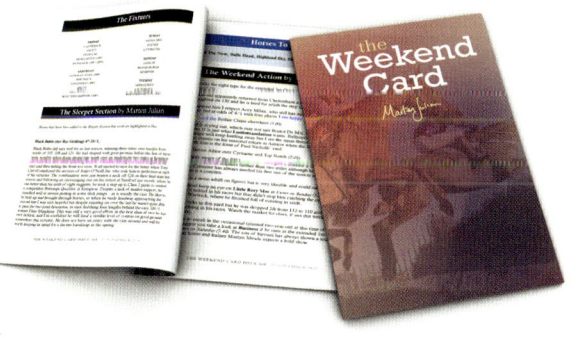

LATEST NEWS ON HORSES FEATURED IN THIS PUBLICATION

WEEKLY RACING INFORMATION!
Packed with over 5000 words of thought-provoking content!

Ten To Follow
Jodie Standing

Jodie has been sufficiently encouraged by the performances of the following horses to believe that they may have more to offer.

ASTIGAR (5YO GREY GELDING)

TRAINER:	David Pipe
PEDIGREE:	No Risk At All – Sissi De Teille (Martaline)
FORM:	22P2 -
OPTIMUM TRIP:	2m 4f +
GROUND:	Soft

Out of a half-sister to the very smart staying chaser and stable companion, Ramses De Teillee, Astigar can only improve as he matures and will surely flourish when his stamina is truly tested.

The good-looking grey produced some smart form last season and forced Neil Mulholland's useful handicap hurdler, Solwara One, to pull out all the stops on his racecourse debut in a bumper at Uttoxeter last November.

Switched to hurdles for a maiden over 2m 1f at Exeter in the new year, he was only denied by a half-length by the now 129-rated Patroclus, travelling strongly in a prominent position and hitting the front after the penultimate flight before being worn down on the run-in despite staying on willingly at the one pace. The form of that race could hardly have worked out better with the winner, third, fourth, fifth, seventh and 11th all winning subsequently.

Pulled up on a revisit to Exeter in February when ridden with more restraint on the terrible ground, he then returned to something like his best on good to soft ground at Plumpton in March when upped in trip to an extended 2m 4f. His jumping left a little to be desired on that occasion but he probably found the track tighter than ideal and was eventually beaten only eight lengths by the 135-rated Smurphy Enki.

Attractively rated on a mark of 123, Astigar has the option of sticking to novice races or dipping his toe into handicap company. Whatever connections choose to do, the gelding has the potential to progress into an above average type. I'll be disappointed if he isn't contesting Graded races by the end of the season.

CHAMP KIELY (5YO BAY GELDING)

TRAINER: WILLIE MULLINS
PEDIGREE: OCOVANGO – CREGG SO (MOSCOW SOCIETY)
FORM: U - 1
OPTIMUM TRIP: 2M 4F +
GROUND: SOFT

There are many potentially useful young horses in Willie Mullins stable, some which have a bigger reputation than others, and although Champ Kiely has shown tremendous promise, I hope he slips into the under the radar category.

The son of Ocovango was a major eye-catcher on his pointing debut for Pat Doyle at Dromahane back in December 2020 where he made swift progress from mid division and loomed on to the scene at the third from home only to get in too tight to the fence and land awkwardly, causing him to unseat his jockey.

That was a good standard maiden and the second and third have shown promise under Rules for Olly Murphy and Lucinda Russell respectively, whilst the fourth won on his bumper debut.

Champ Kiely was sold privately to Willie Mullins and Miss M A Masterson following the run and he made an instant impact in a bumper at Limerick, only winning by half a length but it was more the manner with which he travelled through the race that was impressive.

Taking a strong hold for nearly all the race, Jody Townend did well to hold on to him for as long as she did before he pulled his way to the front over half a mile from home. Still on the bridle entering the straight, he'd be forgiven for not finding much when challenged by the eventual runner-up inside the final two furlongs, but it says plenty about the engine he possesses, that not only was he able to stay on strongly, but he upped the tempo quite considerably up the run-in and probably won with far more in hand than the margin of victory suggests.

A big, raw individual with plenty of room for physical development, he looks a very exciting youngster with the talent to go far. If he learns to settle, he should stay further than 2m 4f, given he's a half-brother to a 2m 5f chase winner and his dam is a half-sister to Marufo who stayed 3m 2f.

DHOWIN (7YO BAY GELDING)

TRAINER: WARREN GREATREX
PEDIGREE: YEATS – ON THE WAY HOME (FLEMENSFIRTH)
FORM: 52/614/635F4 -
OPTIMUM TRIP: 2M 4F – 3M
GROUND: SOFT

Dhowin is one of the more exposed horses in my ten to follow, but I believe we have yet to see the best from him.

The seven-year-old started his career with Jonjo O'Neill for whom he had five starts, including two bumpers and three hurdles, winning once at Hereford over an extended 2m 3f on soft ground before selling as part of the late Trevor Hemmings' dispersal sale for £40,000 last September.

He then made his debut for his current connections in a handicap hurdle over 2m 4f at Wincanton in November, finishing sixth after travelling smoothly towards the rear and keeping on gradually for gentle pressure despite lacking fluency over his flights.

That was from a mark of 123 on ground probably quicker than ideal (good to soft) but he shaped with even greater promise on soft ground at Ascot the following month when stepped up in trip to an extended 2m 5f from a mark of 120. Again, he travelled smoothly and mounted a strong challenge entering the home straight despite being slightly hampered on the bend. Keeping on at the one pace over the final couple of flights, he was only beaten two and a half lengths by Emir Sacree.

His best race of the season was arguably his 11-length beating into fifth in the Listed Lanzarote Handicap Hurdle at Kempton from a mark of 123. At the time I felt the tight track would be against him, and that appeared to be the case for most of the race as he travelled in snatches until staying on with purpose down the straight to finish within 11 lengths of Boreham Bill.

Remarkably, the handicapper left his mark unchanged, and I really fancied him next time at Newbury in February when upped in trip to 3m, but after being well supported in the betting, he overjumped the first flight of hurdles and exited the race. He then returned to the same course and distance the following month, and once again was strong in the market but he probably found the good spring ground against him and could only finish fourth despite receiving a tremendous ride by Caoilin Quinn.

I strongly believe we'll see the best of Dhowin on a galloping track over 2m 5f–3m on soft ground. He's a powerful horse with great scope for fences and I'm sure he'll excel in handicaps this term.

DREAMS OF HOME (5YO BAY GELDING)

TRAINER: DONALD MCCAIN
PEDIGREE: JET AWAY – KNOCKTARTAN (KING'S RIDE)
FORM: 1111 -
OPTIMUM TRIP: 2M 4F +
GROUND: SOFT

Donald McCain has a handful of novice chasers with Graded potential and Dreams Of Home is right amongst them.

The five-year-old son of Jet Away produced an electric round of jumping when making all to beat Bill Baxter by a length in a maiden point-to-point at Moira last October and that form worked out very well with the runner-up scoring by 13 lengths in a Fakenham bumper on his Rules debut for Warren Greatrex. The third has also since won three times.

Purchased privately by current connections following that victory, Dreams Of Home made an impressive winning debut for Donald McCain at Wetherby in January in a 2m maiden hurdle run on heavy ground. Taken to the front from the second flight of hurdles, the bay jumped OK – not as impressively as his point – and pulled clear of the field up the straight, finding plenty under pressure on the run-in despite landing flat-footed over the last.

That success was followed by another victory, this time over a furlong further at Carlisle where he lowered the colours of Royal Arcade to the tune of three and three-quarter lengths, with the runner-up highlighting the form on his next start when winning by 25 lengths over the same course and distance.

Dreams Of Home then rounded off a fine campaign with a nine-length beating of subsequent winner Coolkill in a modestly contested novices' hurdle at Newcastle where he proved he could handle good to soft ground, having previously raced on soft or heavy going.

A half-brother to Katy Price's stable stalwart Minellacelebration who stayed 3m 2f from the family of the smart staying chaser Ad Hoc. There's every reason to suggest Dreams Of Home can not only improve for a fence, but relish the test of the larger obstacles, especially once upped in trip beyond 2m 4f.

ESCARIA TEN (7YO BAY GELDING)

TRAINER: Gordon Elliott
PEDIGREE: Maresca Sorrento – Spartes Eria (Ballingarry)
FORM: 1/23110/5123P -
OPTIMUM TRIP: 3m +
GROUND: Soft

Escaria Ten is a name many of you will have heard of, but I believe we're just starting to see his true potential.

The seven-year-old joined Gordon Elliott after staying on strongly to win a point-to-point at Borris House in March 2019 and finished second to The Little Yank on his bumper debut at Tipperary in October later that year, a race which proved an insufficient test of stamina.

Quickly switched to hurdles and upped in trip to 2m 4f at Fairyhouse in November 2019 he finished a very good third behind Diol Ker, with Monkfish splitting the two, and then went on to win twice over 3m at Cork and Ayr respectively in the colours of the McNeill family in January 2020 having been sold through the ring for £100,000 the previous month.

He signed off his first season under Rules by finishing down the field in the Martin Pipe Conditional Jockeys' Handicap Hurdle at the 2020 Cheltenham Festival from a mark of 136. I strongly fancied his chances there but a combination of the shorter trip and quicker ground saw him too far out of his comfort zone.

A switch to fences last season brought further success and he returned the impressive 20-length winner of a beginners chase at Thurles over 3m 1f on soft ground in December, jumping well and cruising through the race before pulling effortlessly clear in the latter stages. He then went on to finish a good second to Eklat De Rire in a Grade 3 novice chase over the same distance at Naas the next month, this time plugging on at the one pace without ever threatening the winner having made a blunder at the fifth from home.

His best effort to date was probably his excellent third to Galvin in the Grade 2 National Hunt Chase at the Cheltenham Festival. Always well positioned throughout, Adrian Heskin gave him a near-perfect ride, helping him at his fences when needed and producing him to win the race at the right time. Leading over the second from home, I expected him to pull away up the hill, but Galvin had a bit up his sleeve and passed him after the last; he was then collared on the hill by the rallying Next Destination and eventually crossed the line just three lengths behind the winner.

Escaria Ten – a potential National winner?

He then signed off the season at Fairyhouse in the Irish Grand National, where it was probably a case of a bridge too far after a tough race the previous month.

This season I believe he'll be going close in a National, whether it be a Welsh, English, Irish or maybe Scottish, if the ground were to be soft enough. He's a dour stayer with a touch of class and the stronger, more mature he gets, the better he'll become. A mark of 151 is fair on what he's achieved, but I hope there's more to come.

GARS DE SCEAUX (5YO GREY GELDING)

TRAINER: Gordon Elliott
PEDIGREE: Saddler Maker – Replique (April Night)
FORM: 1/211 -
OPTIMUM TRIP: 3m +
GROUND: Soft

Gordon Elliott and J P McManus surely won't be wasting too much time over hurdles with this exciting novice chase prospect.

The imposing grey son of Saddler Maker more than likely found the 2m trip a shade too sharp when beaten 12 lengths by Hook Up on his hurdling debut at Fairyhouse last November and appreciated the step up to 2m 4f when battling bravely to shed his maiden tag at Navan in January. The fourth, fifth, seventh and 11th have all since given that form some shape by winning in the summer months.

Upped in trip again, this time to 2m 7f on a revisit to Navan in March, Gars De Sceaux proved far too good for the opposition and returned home the very easy nine-length winner, sluicing through the mud and coming clear after the third from home to win in a canter.

From the family of Bristol De Mai, Gars De Sceaux is every inch a staying chaser.

He'll likely start off in an ordinary novice chase, but I expect him to compete at the festivals throughout the season and it's not beyond the realms of possibility for him to end up in the Brown Advisory Novices' Chase or the National Hunt Chase come March, for which he's best priced 33/1 and 40/1 respectively.

JOURNEY WITH ME (5YO CHESTNUT GELDING)

TRAINER: HENRY DE BROMHEAD
PEDIGREE: MAHLER – KILBARRY DEMON (BOB'S RETURN)
FORM: 11 -
OPTIMUM TRIP: 2M 4F +
GROUND: SOFT

Journey With Me is unexposed, but he's already a name on many people's lips.

The chestnut son of Mahler created a stir when getting off the mark with the minimal amount of fuss in a four-year-old maiden point at Ballindenisk last November for handler Michael Murphy, jumping with aplomb at the head of affairs and coming home the easy 12-length winner from Gentleman De Mai, with a further 18 lengths back to the third, who has since performed to a modest level under Rules.

After joining Henry de Bromhead in the colours of Robcour, Journey With Me went on to win the 2m 2f point-to-point bumper at Gowran Park in March – a race with an illustrious roll of honour with previous winners including Yorkhill, Minella Melody and Bob Olinger, all subsequent Cheltenham Festival winners.

Prominent throughout, as he was in his point, the Mahler gelding cruised through the race and entered the home straight seemingly in a hack canter before crossing the line without coming off the bridle, 13 lengths clear of Galudon.

Visually, the performance could not have been more impressive, and he's already quoted at 16/1 for the Ballymore Novices' Hurdle and 25/1 for the Albert Bartlett Novices' Hurdle.

To the eye, he looks a dour stayer and copes well with testing ground, but given he's a half-brother to Yorkist, who won over 2m–2m 3f, Drunken Counsel who won a bumper and Bull Ride who won over 2m, there's enough to suggest the five-year-old may have enough speed to contest intermediate trips this season before stepping up in distance next term.

He has the potential to dine at the top table.

PILOT SHOW (4YO BAY GELDING)

TRAINER: WARREN GREATREX
PEDIGREE: YEATS – CASTLE JANE (WESTERNER)
FORM: 1 -
OPTIMUM TRIP: 2M 4F +
GOING: SOFT

Here's a name that not many will have heard of.

Pilot Show was purchased as a foal by trainer Tom Weston for €9,000 back in November 2017 and raised to win a three-mile maiden point-to-point at Garthorpe in April prior to being sold for £45,000 to Highflyer Bloodstock at the Goffs UK Spring Sale the following month.

Ground conditions were probably quicker than ideal when drying out to good to firm from the initial good (watered). Nevertheless, Pilot Show travelled strongly throughout the race and made headway to chase the leaders on the final circuit before moving up to challenge down the back straight. Jumping into a share of the lead at the third from home, he then quickened on the downhill bend into the straight but made a terrible blunder at the penultimate fence when idling.

Strongly ridden, the gelding recovered well but was awfully green on the run to the last and dived over the fence before somehow managing to stay in front all the way to the line to win by a diminishing three parts of a length from Go On Chez.

That horse has since given no end of boosts to the form – winning three times, including twice under Rules for Oliver Greenall. The fifth, Forty Acres, gave further substance to the form by winning his next start.

Pilot Show is a strongly built model who looks to possess a great deal of stamina despite being a half-brother to Castle Keep who showed promise in a bumper. We may not see the best of Pilot Show for another season, but he has raw ability and is likely to slip under the radar. He'll be of particular interest over 2m 4f when encountering soft ground.

STONE MAD (5YO BAY GELDING)

TRAINER: Martin Brassil
PEDIGREE: Yeats – Connaught Hall (Un Desperado)
FORM: 0
OPTIMUM TRIP: 2m +
GROUND: Soft

Stone Mad isn't an obvious inclusion in a ten-to-follow list, but I hope he will pay his way.

The five-year-old son of Yeats topped the Land Rover Sale in 2019 when selling the way of Martin Brassil for €185,000 and made his racecourse debut in a bumper at the Punchestown Festival – a race connections had previously won with Longhouse Poet. You Raised Me Up also finished fourth in the race in 2018.

Tongue-tied and ridden by Derek O'Connor, the gelding attracted strong market support before the off but could only manage to finish eighth, making modest headway entering the straight and keeping on under minimal pressure having been held up in the rear of mid-division.

That was a hot race for a debutant, but I liked the way he travelled in his comfort zone before the tempo increased. The form has also worked out well with the winner bolting up on his hurdling bow at Punchestown this October. The fifth, 12th and 13th also came out and won.

Stone Mad is a brother to the Listed Bumper and useful 2m-2m2f hurdle/chase winner Tintangle and also a half-brother to Tombstone (rated 148 in his pomp).

He's already shown sufficient promise to suggest he has more to give.

TIMELESS BEAUTY (6YO BAY MARE)

TRAINER: Fergal O'Brien
PEDIGREE: Yeats – Love Divided (King's Ride)
FORM: 4/1/353143 -
OPTIMUM TRIP: 2m 4f +
GROUND: Soft/heavy

Timeless Beauty should find improvement as she embarks on a chasing career.

The daughter of Yeats produced a strong staying performance to get off the mark at the second time of asking in the pointing field in February 2020, jumping confidently to touch down in front over the penultimate fence before pulling clear and galloping on relentlessly to the line to record a comfortable three-length success.

Purchased by the McNeill family for £100,000, she made her Rules debut for Warren Greatrex in a novices' hurdle over 2m 4f at Aintree last November, shaping with encouragement and leading the field for a long way before tiring after the last and eventually crossing the line 20 lengths adrift of Wilde About Oscar. She then made no impression next time at Exeter when upped in distance to 2m 7f but ran better than the margin of defeat suggests when beaten 36 lengths behind Ballycallan Fame at Wetherby over an extended 2m 3f on Boxing Day.

Back up in distance to an extended 2m 5f on handicap debut in a mares only race at Ayr in January, she made good use of an opening mark of 99 and ploughed through the heavy ground to record an easy six-and-a-half-length victory from Charm Offensive. She failed to follow up from a 10lb higher mark at Sandown in February but shaped OK when third of 10 back at Ayr in March.

Now rated on a mark of 107, she has been switched to Fergal O'Brien's yard and will most likely embark on a chase campaign. With great scope for fences, I believe she will thrive this season, especially when the mud is flying.

The Irish Contingent
Ronan Groome

For so many racing fans, this is the most exciting time of the year. The air feels a little chillier, the evenings are a little darker, the ground a little softer and the anticipation gauge for our favourite jumpers is now gradually starting to get a little higher.

The dreams are still alive for everyone – trainers, owners, jockeys and punters. Every bet is live now and while it can only really go downhill from here, we're all bang up for the ride.

It's a true privilege to be able to write a 'jumps horses to follow' list in a publication such as this, one of the true pleasures of the profession. I've concentrated on Irish-based horses, with the British sector well covered elsewhere. So here goes:

ASPIRE TOWER
Henry de Bromhead

The one problem at this time of year is trying to decipher which way connections are going to go with their horses.

Aspire Tower could go chasing or stay hurdling (which seems more likely according to a few whispers on Twitter), but he remains an exciting prospect whatever he does. As a rule, I think you can nearly write off the season for a four year old hurdler going on five. It's very difficult for them to tackle their elders in open company and it takes an exceptional one to be competitive and win at Grade 1 level.

Aspire Tower was more than competitive last season. He turned over Abacadabras at Down Royal, finished second to Sharjah in the Matheson Hurdle at Leopardstown and finished fourth in the Champion Hurdle. I think he can now take a big step forward.

The fact he won first time out last term bodes well for his first target this season so keep an eye out for wherever he goes. The Fighting Fifth could be an option given his trainer won the race with Identity Thief in 2015.

If indeed he does go chasing, he will be of as much interest, considering his size and proven two-mile speed. He would be a logical Arkle contender.

Aspire Tower – all options still open

CAPE GENTLEMAN
Emmet Mullins

Emmet Mullins is becoming more and more of a force in National Hunt racing and one of his star names is Cape Gentleman, who has the scope to improve further this season.

The son of Champs Elysees won the Irish Cesarewitch last year and while he was a smooth winner of his maiden hurdle over 2m 4f, it was over two miles that he showed his best form. Having been pulled up in the 2m 6f Grade 1 novice hurdle at the Dublin Racing Festival, he appeared again just three weeks later, winning the Dovecote impressively at Kempton over two miles.

He went back to the Flat this summer and finished a four-length fifth in the Ascot Stakes before again showing his prowess over the minimum hurdles trip when third in the Galway Hurdle. He clearly has the gears for two miles over hurdles, and the Greatwood will surely be on his agenda given his trainer won that race last season with The Shunter.

Going forward, he will be interesting back up in trip over hurdles, given the stamina he has shown at a very high level over staying trips on the Flat.

With that in mind, it's not a ridiculous suggestion to say he could end up being a Stayers' Hurdle horse.

Cape Gentleman – one for the Stayers' Hurdle?

CROSSED MY MIND
Arthur Moore

There could be a big handicap chase win in Crossed My Mind this season. Arthur Moore's nine-year-old, owned by J P McManus, remains lightly raced and looks capable of scoring at least once off his current mark of 132.

He started off his season with two wins last term, notably running out an impressive winner of the Grade B Foxrock Handicap Chase over 2m 4f at Navan which could be his target again. However, his run in the Grade A Leopardstown Handicap Chase at the Dublin Racing Festival really caught the eye. Nothing travelled better going into the straight and he looked set to play a leading role after jumping the last alongside Livelovelaugh only for his effort to peter out on the run-in.

That race was over an extended 2m 5f and it might have just stretched his stamina. What's more, the form of the race could hardly have worked out better given Minella Times, Livelovelaugh, Farclas and Scoir Mear all went on to prosper significantly in their next races.

Crossed My Mind will be interesting now in handicap chases at 2m 4f or below – indeed he may even have the speed to come down to 2m 1f or thereabouts, which could open more doors for him.

ECHOES IN RAIN
Willie Mullins

It's difficult to find Willie Mullins-trained dark horses because not many go under the radar.

I'm not suggesting Echoes In Rain is one that nobody will have heard of – she was of course a Grade 1 winner at Punchestown – but she might still be a little underrated, and may continue to be during the season, with her trainer liable to keep her to mares' company.

Despite always running freely and giving her riders a torrid time, she won four of her five starts last season and rounded her year off with that Grade 1 win over 2m at Punchestown. That form doesn't amount to much and she didn't look impressive, coming off a steady pace in a small field, but she got the job done when things weren't run to suit her and that bodes well.

She is much better judged on her penultimate effort at Fairyhouse, where she slammed stable companion M C Muldoon by 15 lengths in a Grade 2 contest. That race was run at a hectic gallop, so it definitely helped her, and the time she clocked was excellent, a whole eight seconds faster than the preceding maiden hurdle and also comparing favourably with the Grade 1 run over two and a half miles later on the card.

She may well be kept to her own sex for much of the season – that's the Willie Mullins modus operandi with mares – but she will be of most interest if given a chance in a Grade 1 field and/or racing off a fast pace over two miles, which could be in a big handicap hurdle.

Given her tendency to run freely, she's likely to stick to two miles, and that means the Champion Hurdle could be on her radar. She's only a five-year-old, with just five runs over hurdles, and she is with the best trainer of a National Hunt mare ever.

She has huge potential.

GAILLARD DU MESNIL
Willie Mullins

I'm going to follow the Ballymore Novices' Hurdle form all season because I think it could be one of the best renewals in recent times and history shows the 2m 5f contest is usually an excellent guide to finding the best horses around in any division.

Bob Olinger won it comfortably in the end and he'll be a leading player whatever he does this term, but I was taken by the run of Gaillard Du Mesnil in second.

Willie Mullins's five-year-old looked to be outpaced as he moved up beside the winner and Bravemansgame turning for home, but it was really impressive the way he recharged himself and ultimately outstayed the third coming up the hill.

Prior to that he'd won the 2m 6f Grade 1 novice hurdle on testing ground at the Dublin Racing Festival in impressive fashion, very much suggesting that three miles would be within his compass.

After the Ballymore, Willie Mullins was of the opinion that Gaillard Du Mesnil would be going chasing and up in trip. With his proven class against two of the best novice hurdlers around at the Festival, he has to be one of the top novice chase prospects for the season.

GARS DE SCEAUX
Gordon Elliott

Gars De Sceaux is another one that was probably in bonus territory last season because he looks every inch a chaser and will be of significant interest over fences this term.

Gordon Elliott's five-year-old got off the mark when upped in trip to 2m 4f at Navan. That form was nothing special but he was a far more comfortable winner when nine lengths too good for his rivals over 2m 7f at the same track in March. Both of those wins came on testing ground, which may be important to him, but he hasn't really been tested on a decent surface yet and he is completely unexposed over three miles, which really could be the making of him.

Connections may well feel the benefit of being patient with this son of Saddler Maker, who coincidentally beat his now useful stablemate Magic Tricks in a Borris House point-to-point before making his move to Cullentra House.

GENTLEMAN JOE
Henry de Bromhead

This three-year-old son of Authorized has been bought by Robcour out of Joseph Tuite's yard in Lambourn and goes into training with Henry de Bromhead.

He looked smart winning a one-mile maiden at Kempton last March before running a little disappointingly when well held in the Feilden Stakes at Newmarket. That may have come too soon for him, given it was just his third run, and he was much better when third to Lone Eagle in the Cocked Hat Stakes at Goodwood on his next and final run in Britain.

The form of that Listed contest could hardly have worked out better given the subsequent exploits of the winner and runner-up Yibir, while the next two horses that finished in behind him, Aleas and Stay Well, both won on their next starts, in Listed and handicap company respectively.

Henry de Bromhead has done well with recruits from the Flat in Britain, most notably Aspire Tower (also mentioned in this list) and without doubt Gentleman Joe has the potential to make an impact in juvenile hurdles.

He is 33/1 for the Triumph Hurdle.

HARRY ALONZO
Noel Meade

This five-year-old gelding was one of the most impressive regulation bumper winners of last season when he won at Leopardstown's Christmas Festival.

Ridden by Pat Taaffe, the son of Montmartre came off the bridle early enough but responded really well, almost too well, because he swept by the leaders on the turn into the straight and found himself in front plenty early enough. Challenged by Gordon Elliott's well-fancied Top Bandit, he looked a bit of a sitting duck, but it was to his credit that he readily held off that rival and by the end of the race he was pulling away again.

It wasn't a surprise that J P McManus swooped in to buy him after this race and he only ran once again, when second to Letsbeclearaboutit in a good bumper at Fairyhouse. There was absolutely no shame in that result because that Gavin Cromwell-trained horse was one of the best bumper horses in Ireland last season, whose only defeats came to Sir Gerhard and Kilcruit.

The way he races, Harry Alonzo could prosper over 2m 4f in time and it would be no surprise to see him run in some of the good novice hurdles at Navan in the run-up to Christmas, as his trainer loves to go well at his local track.

JUMPING JET
Gordon Elliott

It doesn't yet seem to be common knowledge that Jumping Jet has been bought by Robcour and is now in training with Gordon Elliott.

She is 33/1 for the Mares' Novices' Hurdle and when it does become known she has moved to Cullentra House, it's unlikely those fancy prices will remain available.

Previously trained by Barry Fitzgerald, she won a Gowran Park mares' bumper by all of 29 lengths on her sole start last March, perhaps revelling in the soft ground conditions. That sort of form should be treated with caution but promisingly, both the second and third mares came out and won comfortably on their next starts which added some solidity to the performance of the winner.

She may need soft ground and it could turn out that performance wasn't as good as it looks, but whatever way you weigh it up, she is very exciting and will be a real force in the mares' novice hurdle division through the winter.

MR INCREDIBLE
Henry de Bromhead

There probably wasn't a better maiden hurdle run all season than the 2m 4f contest in which Mr Incredible finished second at Leopardstown last Christmas.

In taking the runner-up position, the son of Westerner split Gaillard Du Mesnil and Magic Daze, the latter subsequently winning a Grade 1 at the same track, and both going on to be placed at the Cheltenham Festival.

That was Mr Incredible's first experience of the track and he duly got the job done on his second start in impressive fashion, turning over the well-regarded Willie Mullins-trained mare Glens Of Antrim at Naas.

He didn't run again last season and given he was described by his trainer as "a real chasing type", it's likely connections decided to hold fire with him and save him for this term. A beautiful-looking horse, he may be best on soft ground and could well be a force to be reckoned with over trips from 2m 4f upwards.

The Bumpers
Jodie Standing

Jodie has spotted sufficient promise in the following horses to warrant inclusion in this feature.

ARTHUR'S SEAT (4YO BAY GELDING)

TRAINER:	Keith Dalgleish
PEDIGREE:	Champs Elysees – Sojitzen (Great Journey)
FORM:	1221 -
OPTIMUM TRIP:	2m +
GROUND:	Soft

This gelding is more exposed than most but looks a fantastic prospect for novice hurdles.

Arthur's Seat travelled strongly and scooted clear to win easily on his racecourse debut in a 'junior' bumper over an extended 1m 5f at Huntingdon last September and cemented that promise under a 7lb penalty over a similar distance at Doncaster when pipped by Alan King's Masaccio in November.

Second again, this time over an extended 1m 7f at Musselburgh in January, he stayed on strongly from well off the pace to chase home the well-regarded Donald McCain Rules debutant Fruit N Nut before rounding off a solid campaign with a one-length victory over subsequent winner Dynamite Kentucky at Kelso the following month, again strong at the line despite the testing conditions.

Closely related to a 5f two-year-old winner, Arthur's Seat belies his pedigree and has plenty of frame to fill. Still only four, he ought to have summered well and a successful season over hurdles can be expected. He shapes like a horse who will stay further than two miles.

Arthur's Seat – a useful prospect for novice hurdles

BILL BAXTER (5YO GREY GELDING)

TRAINER: Warren Greatrex
PEDIGREE: Milan – Blossom Rose (Roselier)
FORM: 214 -
OPTIMUM TRIP: 2m 4f +
GROUND: Soft

A stoutly bred individual that should improve significantly when stepped up in trip.

Bill Baxter stayed on well to finish within a length of Dreams Of Home in a four-year-olds' maiden point-to-point at Moira last October – form which worked out extremely well with the winner subsequently unbeaten in three starts under Rules and is now rated on a mark of 134 for Donald McCain. The third has also won three times since joining Joseph O'Brien.

Purchased privately by current connections, the grey made his bumper debut at Fakenham in January where he travelled wide throughout but moved through to dispute the lead on the bridle at the halfway point. Effortlessly drawing clear inside the final three furlongs, he crossed the line with 13 lengths to spare over the second, who has since won twice.

Tried in Listed company at Newbury in February, he ran a good race to finish fourth, staying on well in the closing stages to be beaten just shy of nine lengths by Good Risk At All with I Like To Move It (ninth in the Champion Bumper) and Gelino Bello (winner on debut) splitting the two.

With close relations who won over trips up to 3m 1f, more improvement should be unlocked when his stamina comes into play. He copes well with testing ground.

DALAMOI (4YO BAY GELDING)

TRAINER: Tim Vaughan
PEDIGREE: Pour Moi – Dalamine (Sillery)
FORM: 2 -
OPTIMUM TRIP: 2m 4f +
GROUND: Soft

This is a nicely bred type who showed abundant promise on his sole start.

Dalamoi fought all the way to the line when denied by only a neck by the fellow newcomer, Revasser, on his bumper debut at Warwick in April. Settled in the pack and travelling smoothly for most of the race, he was last off the bridle turning for home but showed a tendency to lug to his left under pressure and couldn't quite raise an effort to overhaul the winner despite holding the fast-finishing third – who was benefiting from experience – by three parts of a length at the line.

A half-brother to five winners including the high-class stayer Don Poli and Debece (won five times for Tim Vaughan), Dalamoi should thrive with the passing of time.

With the physique to be a chaser, the potential for this gelding holds no limits and he will benefit for a step up in trip, probably on softer ground.

DOYEN DU BAR (5YO BAY GELDING)

TRAINER: Pauline Robson
PEDIGREE: Doyen – Hollygrove Native (Be My Native)
FORM: 1 -
OPTIMUM TRIP: 2m +
GROUND: Soft

This is one of the most exciting performers for a lower profile yard.

Well backed on his bumper debut at Carlisle in March, Pauline Robson's gelding was smuggled away towards the rear of the field and travelled powerfully throughout in the hands of Henry Brooke.

Pulled wide approaching the turn for home, the five-year-old passed his rivals with ease and cruised into contention on the bridle halfway up the hill before finding a useful turn of foot in the soft ground to draw clear in impressive fashion in the closing stages, eventually crossing the line with six and a half widening lengths to Bert Wilson.

That was only a modest bumper, which has not worked out well, but the visual impression was striking.

Closely related to Royal Native, who stayed 3m 1f, out of a dam who placed up to 2m 6f. Doyen Du Bar looks a very exciting prospect, who has both speed and stamina.

FLAME BEARER (6YO BAY GELDING)

TRAINER: Pat Doyle
PEDIGREE: Fame And Glory – Banba (Docksider)
FORM: 2/11 -
OPTIMUM TRIP: 2m
GROUND: Soft

A keen goer with the potential to be a Graded performer over hurdles.

Flame Bearer shaped like a nice sort when finishing second – jumping let him down – on his sole point-to-point for Donnchadh Doyle and sported a tongue-tie when making an instant impression on Rules debut in a bumper at Thurles in December for Pat Doyle.

Taking a keen hold, he cruised through the race and pulled clear inside the final couple of furlongs to record a comfortable five-length success. He then proved that effort was no fluke by following up under a penalty at Limerick in March, again taking a hold and powering through the race before pulling clear up the home straight to win by three and a half lengths, with any amount more still in hand.

Related to several Flat performers, this six-year-old clearly possesses a huge engine and has the potential to go far providing his keenness can be channelled correctly. Testing ground suits well, although connections have said he will go on anything.

GUARDINO (5YO BROWN GELDING)

TRAINER: BEN PAULING
PEDIGREE: AUTHORIZED – MONICKER (MANDURO)
FORM: 2/31 -
OPTIMUM TRIP: 2M
GROUND: GOOD

Guardino looks a great prospect for the two-mile hurdle division.

The attractive son of Authorized showed up well when filling second place in a point-to-point at Oldtown in February 2020 but was only third when well backed on bumper debut for current connections at Carlisle last November.

Attempting to make all, he moved strongly on the front end and kicked on at the bottom of the hill but faded tamely over a furlong from home, eventually crossing eight and a half lengths behind Aviewtosea. It was later reported that he'd produced a dirty trachea wash.

Given a break, he appreciated the speed test of a bumper at Kempton in February and produced a smart turn of foot off the home bend before keeping on in admirable style to win by a neck under Nico De Boinville.

By Authorized out of a Manduro mare and related to winners on the Flat from 6.5f to 1m 4f. This is surely one for the two-mile programme.

He could be smart.

HILLCREST (6YO BROWN GELDING)

TRAINER: Henry Daly
PEDIGREE: Stowaway – Shop Dj (Dushyantor)
FORM: 21 -
OPTIMUM TRIP: 2m 4f +
GROUND: Good to Soft

This son of Stowaway is an embryonic chaser if ever there was one.

Given his imposing stature, it's of little surprise that Hillcrest didn't make his debut until he was six years old. That was at Doncaster in January where he lobbed along in the mid division on the outside of the field before progressing into a prominent position at the top of the straight. Green under pressure and hanging, he stuck on in game fashion all the way to the line and was only denied by a nose by Nicky Henderson's Wiseguy.

Hillcrest then went to Wetherby and looked booked for a place at best at the top of the home straight but given time to find his stride under Brian Hughes and helped by the strong tempo of the race which etched into his stamina, the scopey gelding stayed on strongly passing through the wings of the final flight hurdles and powered up the run-in to collar Armand De Brignac in the shadows of the post to win by a neck.

Sold for €190,000 as a store horse and out of the smart race mare Shop Dj who won seven times for Peter Fahey, including a Grade 3 over hurdles, Hillcrest will be suited by a stiffer test of stamina, but it won't be until he tackles fences in seasons to come that we see his true potential.

HOB HOUSE (4YO BAY GELDING)

TRAINER: Nicky Henderson
PEDIGREE: Walk In The Park – Tante Sissi (Lesotho)
FORM: 1 -
OPTIMUM TRIP: 2m
GROUND: Good to Soft

A once-raced J P McManus-owned gelding out of a half-sister to Champion Hurdle winner Epatante.

Hooded for bumper debut at Southwell in March, the gelding took a keen hold at the head of affairs but always oozed class, and once briefly joined for the lead turning for home, he gradually reasserted his advantage and found plenty for pressure before keeping on well under hands and heels riding to win by a comfortable one and a quarter lengths.

Hob House is unlikely to represent much value for betting purposes, but this is an individual open to any amount of progress and could develop into a top-class prospect over hurdles, provided his trainer can keep a lid on the gelding's enthusiasm.

HUNTERS YARN (4YO BAY GELDING)

TRAINER: Willie Mullins
PEDIGREE: Fame And Glory – Full Of Birds (Epervier Bleu)
FORM: 31 -
OPTIMUM TRIP: 2m +
GROUND: Soft

This well-related type now resides at Willie Mullins for owners Simon Munir & Isaac Souede.

Hunters Yarn was unsuited by the slow tempo of the race when making his debut in a bumper at Naas for Pat Doyle in February but stayed on eye-catchingly well into third place crossing the line despite meeting with plenty of trouble in the latter stages.

Sporting a first-time tongue-tie the following month at Thurles, the four-year-old improved significantly to win by a very easy 17 lengths. Ridden more prominently, he travelled strongly throughout the race and came clear off the home bend to win in the manner of a top prospect.

A full brother to Michael Scudamore's useful 2m hurdler Do Your Job and Noel Meade's bumper winner Highland Charge, he's also a half-brother to Listed winner Down Ace.

There's obvious speed in Hunters Yarn's pedigree but he looks a natural galloper who possesses plenty of stamina. He could be a smart performer.

JUMPING JET (5YO BROWN MARE)

TRAINER: GORDON ELLIOTT
PEDIGREE: GETAWAY – LITTLE MILI (MILAN)
FORM: 1 -
OPTIMUM TRIP: 2M 4F +
GROUND: SOFT

This mare slips into the 'could be anything' bracket.

The daughter of Getaway was an emphatic winner of a bumper over 2m 1f at Gowran Park in March when trained by Barry Fitzgerald. Despite racing freely, she sluiced through the mud and took over from the long-time leader half a mile from home before pulling clear with ease.

Kept up to her work up the home straight, she crossed the line with 29 lengths to spare over Choice Of Words who won next time by 13 lengths and later finished second in a Grade 3 behind Grangee (winner of a Grade 2 and placed sixth in the Champion Bumper).

Out of an unraced half-sister to Dark Sunset, who stayed 3m, and from the family of smart staying chaser Percy Smollett.

Jumping Jet needs to learn to settle but is expected to appreciate a distance of ground.

She starts the new season for Gordon Elliott in the colours of Robcour.

KILBEG KING (6YO BAY GELDING)

TRAINER: Anthony Honeyball
PEDIGREE: Doyen – Prayuwin Drummer (Presenting)
FORM: 2/11 -
OPTIMUM TRIP: 2m 4f +
GROUND: Soft

A wide-margin bumper winner on Midlands National Day at Uttoxeter.

This son of Doyen showed more than a hint of ability when second on pointing debut at Tinahely in January 2020 for Colin Bowe, shaping like the most likely winner until losing all momentum with a misjudged leap at the last when holding a two-length advantage.

Not seen again until November, he returned with a bang to win a maiden at Ballindenisk by eight lengths after being left clear at the last where his nearest pursuer fell when held.

Purchased for £45,000 by current connections, he was well backed when making a winning Rules debut in a bumper at Uttoxeter on good to soft ground in March. Always travelling with ease in the mid pack, he kept on strongly after moving to the front over two furlongs from home and crossed the line to win by seven and a half lengths.

A half-brother to 2m 4f hurdle winner Champagne Noir and related to a 3m performer. He copes well with soft ground and should be better suited to trips that bring his stamina into play.

REVASSER (4YO BAY GELDING)

TRAINER:	Lucy Wadham
PEDIGREE:	Ask – Open Cry (Montelimar)
FORM:	1 -
OPTIMUM TRIP:	2m 4f +
GROUND:	Good to Soft

A stoutly bred gelding from a family the trainer knows exceptionally well.

Revasser overcame significant greenness to make a winning debut in a bumper at Warwick in April. Travelling in snatches, he made headway on the outside of the field under gentle persuasion from Bryony Frost and moved to the front with a furlong to travel. Keeping on tenaciously close home, he held fellow newcomer Dalamoi by a neck with a further three parts of a length back to the more experienced The Odissey.

The four-year-old doesn't possess the most aesthetically pleasing action but he's a three-parts brother to eight-time winner Le Reve, who stayed 3m 5f, (same ownership/trainer combo) and the smart 3m + chaser Join Together.

This gelding did well to show so much over an inadequate test of stamina and should thrive when tackling a distance of ground. His willing attitude is a tremendous asset.

SAINT PATRIC (5YO BAY GELDING)

TRAINER: James Moffatt
PEDIGREE: Universal – Blazing Bay (Luso)
FORM: 60 - 3
OPTIMUM TRIP: 2m +
GROUND: Soft

Saint Patric could slip under the radar for a lower profile base.

The son of Universal shaped with potential when staying on close home into sixth place having been outpaced on his racecourse debut in an all-weather 'newcomers' bumper at Newcastle in January and again showed potential when ridden more prominently the following month at Doncaster. He was leading when ridden at the top of the home straight before fading and eventually crossing the line almost 20 lengths behind Skytastic.

Third when last seen at Perth in June, he made good late headway after being short of room on the run-in and ought to do better now hurdling.

From a family the trainer knows well, being a half-brother to stable companion Lady Bowes (bumper and 2m 4f hurdle winner). From the family of Blazing Sky and Blazing Beacon.

The five-year-old is likely to be placed to good effect around the northern circuit and may benefit for a truer test of stamina.

SHALLWEHAVEONEMORE (4YO BAY GELDING)

TRAINER:	GARY MOORE
PEDIGREE:	AUTHORIZED – PRINCESS ROSEBURG (JOHANNESBURG)
FORM:	1 -
OPTIMUM TRIP:	2M
GROUND:	GOOD

Here's another promising four-year-old that is flying the 'could be anything' flag after an impressive debut success.

Gary Moore's son of Authorized made his debut in a Kempton bumper in March that usually produces some above average performers. Indeed Mister Fisher and Shishkin won here for Nicky Henderson in 2018 and 2019 respectively.

Settled towards the rear, Shallwehaveonemore made steady headway on the turn into the back straight before nipping up the inside of the field and cornering well on the turn for home. Soon on the scene, the gelding quickened smartly on the bridle down the straight and powered past Nicky Henderson's runner before drawing clear inside the final furlong to win by four and a half lengths, with plenty more in hand. It also took an age for Josh Moore to bring the gelding to a stop.

Related to a couple of Flat winners up to 1m 7f and out of a French Listed-placed 5f-7.5f winner.

Shallwehaveonemore has a high cruising speed and a very useful change of gear. He's very much a horse to follow in the two-mile division and, if the early part of the season goes well, it's not beyond the realms of possibility that he could develop into a Supreme Novices' Hurdle candidate.

SOFT RISK (5YO BAY GELDING)

TRAINER: Nicky Richards
PEDIGREE: My Risk – Douce Ambiance (Kouroun)
FORM: 1
OPTIMUM TRIP: 2m +
GROUND: Soft

A hugely exciting prospect to enter the novice hurdle ranks for Nicky Richards.

Soft Risk won in the manner of a smart type on his bumper debut at Ayr in May. Held up in the rear, he made smooth progress to lead inside the final two furlongs before bursting clear with an instant change of gear when asked to put the race to bed and hit the line hard.

The form may not amount to much, but the visual impression was impressive, and the victory came when the yard was going through a quiet spell.

From a predominantly French Flat family out of a half-sister to Group-placed 1m-10.5f winner Melody Blue with further links to a Group 1 winner over 5f.

Soft Risk has tremendous scope and copes well with soft ground but doesn't necessarily need it. He also shapes like he'll stay a trip but his trainer may be in no rush to step up given the copious amount of speed the gelding possesses.

The Champion Hurdle Preview 2022
Marten Julian

Honeysuckle, winner of each of her dozen starts under Rules and her sole point-to-point, is rightly heading the market at a top price of 2/1 for the Champion Hurdle.

Short though this price may seem, given that there are six months for things to go wrong, I confidently expect her to start odds-on to follow up if she gets to post unscathed and with her unbeaten record intact.

Such was her dominance last season that even when she was probably over the top, she was still able to come out at Punchestown in April to win the Paddy Power Champion Hurdle.

As someone who has spent about 50 years trying to find long-priced alternatives to the obvious, I am loath to say it but 2/1 could actually be 'value' for this remarkable mare. At this point in time I would rate Honeysuckle an even-money chance to win the race again.

The mare's talent was evident from the outset, when she beat the useful Annie Mc, now rated on 149 over fences, by 15 lengths in her point-to-point.

She won four times in the 2018/19 season, progressing from a maiden through to Listed, Grade 3 and then Grade 1 company over 2m 4f.

What became apparent through the season was her ability to surge away from the opposition between the last two flights of hurdles.

Honeysuckle – confidently expected to retain her Champion Hurdle crown

She made further progress in 2019/20, beating the males in the Grade 1 Hatton's Grace in December and then showing that she had the tenacity to match her talent when holding the late run of Darver Star, after a protracted tussle with Petit Mouchoir, back at two miles in the Irish Champion Hurdle.

The Champion Hurdle at Cheltenham then became a serious consideration but connections took the easier option and went for the Mares' Hurdle over 2m 4f.

Up against Benie Des Dieux, who was rated 4lb superior, she was ridden handily throughout. Then, approaching the home turn, her rider Rachael Blackmore spotted an opportunity to nip her through a gap on the rails and seize an advantage which stood her in good stead on the run to the line.

Last season she started with a gritty half-length defeat of Ronald Pump in the Hatton's Grace, sticking her neck out bravely to hold the runner-up's late challenge on the run-in.

She then dropped back to two miles for the Irish Champion Hurdle in February. Close up throughout she settled on the outside of the field, travelling smoothly with her head bowed low, until the third last where she moved up alongside the pacesetting Petit Mouchoir.

It was then that her rider allowed her to stride on, shooting five lengths clear, and turning for home she held that advantage over the improving Abacadabras, to cross the line 10 lengths clear of the runner-up.

The race was run in a good time – 2.6 seconds faster than the handicapper in the next, who carried a stone more.

Her jumping, which had at times in the past been a little slipshod, was on this occasion much slicker. Next time in the Champion Hurdle it was her alacrity and speed over the hurdles that impressed – spring-heeled and clearing the early flights with air to spare.

Always handy, never further back than fifth, she was kept to the outside of the field for the first half mile before tucking in and settling about three lengths off the pace.

Shuffled along for just a few strides at the top of the hill, she went into the lead on the turn for home and quickly went clear. Another fine jump at the last sealed the race as she strode away to win by six and a half lengths from Sharjah, who came home three lengths clear of 2020 winner Epatante.

Six weeks later she appeared in the Paddy Power Champion Hurdle at Punchestown.

Once again she was big over the early flights, notably the first and then a little hesitant over the second and fourth. She again overjumped the second last before shooting five lengths clear. At that point the race looked in safekeeping, only for her to appear to slam on the brakes approaching the last and allow Sharjah to get within a couple of lengths, before staying on again to win with little in hand.

Afterwards the jockey attributed the mare's performance to her "feeling the season", with the second reducing the deficit from Cheltenham by just over four lengths.

Honeysuckle again showed at Punchestown that she has the tenacity to match her talent. It's been said many times that top-class horses can overcome adversity and this was the case here.

I can think of no valid reason why any of those that finished behind Honeysuckle at Cheltenham should reverse the form. She holds a clear margin of superiority over her rivals and her rider said after Cheltenham that she was "getting better".

With a clear run through to March she will be very hard to beat and it will take something exceptional from last season's novice generation to steal her crown.

Epatante was at short odds to win the Champion Hurdle for the second year after her impressive seasonal return in the Fighting Fifth.

Her jumping in the 2020 Champion Hurdle, for which she was equipped with earplugs, had been quick and efficient in the main. She clipped the top of a couple of flights and snatched at the third last, but she never lost momentum and travelled smoothly throughout the course of the race.

Produced with a challenge at the last, she put in one of her best leaps and found a change of gear to pull away and beat Sharjah by three lengths.

In doing so she became the fifth of her sex to win the Champion Hurdle, giving Nicky Henderson his eighth winner of the race and owner, JP McManus, his fourth in a row.

Last season started well, with a facile defeat of the talented Sceau Royal in the Fighting Fifth under a ride of supreme confidence from Aidan Coleman. The turn of foot she showed after the last there was breathtaking.

However things did not go according to plan next time in the Christmas Hurdle, where a mistake three from home seemed to unsettle her. In an uneven round she was a little hesitant at the first, big at the second, better at the third and fourth, good at the fifth, clumsy over the sixth and then fine over the last two.

To my eyes she had not looked quite herself from flagfall, never travelling with the ease we have come to expect of her. The trainer says she was subsequently found to have a sore back.

She returned to something close to her best in the Champion Hurdle. Travelling very well from the start, though perhaps a little keen, she jumped efficiently in the main and made progress from the third last, turning for home in fifth about three lengths off the leader.

From that point she made stealthy headway, running on steadily from the last to close the gap on the second and pass the post nine and a half lengths behind the winner.

Six weeks later she met the first two again in the Paddy Power Champion Hurdle but this time finished 12 and a half lengths behind the winner.

Nicky Henderson says that this summer the mare has had "the same surgery as Champ" which he thinks will make a "big difference".

Despite her defeats Epatante still has claim to a very consistent record, with eight wins and only once finishing out of the first three from 13 starts.

She had beaten Sharjah by three lengths in the 2020 Champion Hurdle so it could be argued, on a line through that horse, that there may not be much between her and Honeysuckle at their best.

At 16/1, as opposed to 2/1 for the favourite, and with possible improvement from the medical procedure on her back, a case can be made for a modest saver. She is unlikely to have an alternative target.

Sharjah will probably remain over hurdles.

He has proved a consistent performer at the highest level, tackling Grade 1 company in his last 11 races, but he has four times finished behind Honeysuckle and was still unable to beat her when the mare was below her best at Punchestown in April.

Furthermore he is a year older than Honeysuckle and the only thing that may bring them closer together could be good ground, which suits him better than the mare.

With the race likely to be the target again, the 20/1 each-way is not entirely without appeal. He is usually there or thereabouts.

Abacadabras didn't get a chance to show himself in the Champion Hurdle, tipping over at the third.

He plugged on to finish a 10-length second to Honeysuckle at Leopardstown in February and ended the season beaten 14 lengths by her at Punchestown.

Before that he had overcome a couple of sloppy jumps over the last two flights to beat Buzz over two and a half miles in the Grade 1 Aintree Hurdle. Travelling smoothly in arrears for much of the race, the seven-year-old son of Davidoff cruised through to challenge at the last and had enough in hand to hold the fast-closing runner-up on the run to the line.

On more than one occasion his rider Jack Kennedy, and others before him, have said that he hit the front too soon. That has not been evident to my eyes as he seems to run on stoutly to the line.

Looking back to his novice hurdling days his form could hardly read better, having chased home Envoi Allen at Fairyhouse and run Shishkin to a head in the Supreme at Cheltenham.

The assumption is that he will be campaigned over longer trips this season, or be switched to fences, but he would not be out of place in a Champion Hurdle. His form entitles him to be there or thereabouts.

Bob Olinger, who is quoted at odds ranging from 7/1 to 12/1, is another for whom the future is uncertain.

The six-year-old won his sole start between the flags and then made all to win a 2m 2f bumper at Gowran Park in March 2020.

The following season he returned to Gowran for a 2m maiden hurdle. Travelling well in the lead, he was joined by Ferny Hollow at the second last, who then found a little more from the final flight to win by a length.

Stepped up to 2m 4f for his next two starts, he won a maiden hurdle at Navan by 14 lengths and then beat the useful Blue Lord by six and a half lengths in the Grade 1 Lawlor's Of Naas Novice Hurdle, taking the lead at the second last and drawing away to win cosily.

Just over two months later he was made a well-supported 6/4 favourite to win the 2m 5f Ballymore Novices' Hurdle at Cheltenham.

Racing quite keenly in the early stages, he got close to the fourth last but came there travelling well approaching the second from home. He then drew clear to win by seven and a half lengths from Gaillard Du Mesnil, with the well-regarded Bravemansgame four and a half lengths back in third.

The son of Sholokhov seems likely to go chasing, but he does not lack pace and horses with top-class novice form over two and a half miles have a good record in the Champion Hurdle, so a change of plan may not be entirely out of the question.

There is probably a stronger case for taking the top two-mile hurdle programme with **Appreciate It**, who is a top price of 12/1 for the Champion Hurdle.

The son of Jeremy, who ran third to Envoi Allen on his point-to-point debut in February 2018, won two of his four bumpers culminating with a two-and-a-half-length second to Ferny Hollow at the 2020 Cheltenham Festival.

Switched to hurdling in the autumn, he beat subsequent dual winner Master McShee on his debut at Cork in November and then won two Grade 1s at Leopardstown, beating Irascible by nine lengths in the Paddy Power Future Champions Novice Hurdle over Christmas and Ballyadam by three and a quarter lengths, with Blue Lord in third, in the Chanelle Pharma Novice Hurdle there in February.

Appreciate It – a top contender for the Champion Hurdle

It was on the strength of that fine record that he started 8/11 favourite for the Supreme Novices' Hurdle at Cheltenham. Jumping well, he was always within a few lengths of the leader and took up the running at the second last before going clear to beat Ballyadam by 24 lengths.

After the race trainer Willie Mullins discussed the options for this season, saying that he had thought of Appreciate It as an Arkle prospect and had "never envisioned him for the Champion Hurdle", but then reminded himself that had been the case with Faugheen.

The feature of Appreciate It's performance last season was the ease with which he travelled though his races.

That certainly augurs well for another season of hurdling, but connections will be mindful of the presence of Honeysuckle and their thinking may be swayed by how she gets on this autumn.

You can't mention either Appreciate It or Bob Olinger for the Champion Hurdle without recognising the claims of **Ferny Hollow**, who beat Appreciate It in the Weatherbys Champion Bumper in 2020 and, on his sole start over hurdles last season, beat Bob Olinger at Gowran Park in November.

The six-year-old then met with a setback but was apparently back in training in the spring, with a view to running at Punchestown, only for it to be decided against running him at that late stage.

Ferny Hollow, who comes from the family of Champion Hurdle winners Morley Street and Granville Again, has every right to serious consideration. He has victories over last season's two best novices and having run just once over hurdles has scope for further improvement.

Ferny Hollow – bred to win a Champion Hurdle

One factor that may have a bearing on plans is the prospect of a very strong novice chase division if Appreciate It and Bob Olinger make the switch to fencing.

Much will depend on how things develop through the autumn, but I would not be surprised to see Honeysuckle scare everything away.

No horse, in my view, made greater improvement last spring than the mare **Echoes In Rain**.

The daughter of Authorized, who won twice from five starts for her former trainer on the Flat in France, was beaten 53 lengths on her first start for Willie Mullins on Boxing Day 2019.

She was not seen out again for the best part of 12 months, reappearing with a 15-length success at Naas last December, before getting beaten into fourth by Dreal Deal at Punchestown in January.

A keen-running mare, it was decided to change tactics and hold her up, at which point she started to thrive, winning Grade 2s at Naas in February and Fairyhouse in April, before ending her season with a defeat of Colonel Mustard in a Grade 1 at Punchestown.

The feature of those victories was the change of gear she showed to pull away from her rivals, never more so than in the Grade 2 at Fairyhouse in April, where she quickened away to put 15 lengths between herself and the second between the run to the last and the line.

It was a breathtaking change of gear and hugely impressive on the eye, all the more remarkable given how keen she had been through the course of the race.

The mare's mark of 143 reflects the gulf she has to bridge to compete with the best, and connections will probably opt to keep her to the mares' programme, which the trainer has done with such success in the past.

However she had not stopped improving last spring and she would get an allowance in the Champion Hurdle, albeit the same as Honeysuckle.

I can fully understand why the bookmakers have her priced at a guarded 14/1.

Paul Nicholls will be hoping that **Monmiral** can build on the promise shown last season.

A winner of his sole start in France for Francois Nicolle, when he beat Hell Red – now also with Nicholls – in a 3yr-old hurdle, he went through last season unbeaten, winning on his debut at Exeter in November and then landing a Grade 2, virtually on the bridle, by 11 lengths at Doncaster in December.

He was impressive next time at Haydock, despite a couple of awkward jumps, before ending the campaign with a seven-and-a-half length defeat of Adagio in the Grade 1 Doom Bar Juvenile Hurdle at Aintree. On that occasion he had to dig deep from the last to get the better of the talented runner-up.

Rider Harry Cobden was highly complimentary afterwards, describing him as the "best juvenile I have sat on", adding that he hoped the horse would be switched to fences rather than stay over hurdles.

Monmiral – hurdling or chasing?

It seems, though, that the trainer intends to start the season over hurdles with the Fighting Fifth at Newcastle. That is also the likely target for Epatante, so the outcome is sure to have an early impact on the Champion Hurdle market.

Monmiral still has something to learn about jumping a hurdle but his inexperience was evident through the season and he has ample scope for improvement.

It should be noted, at this point, that Monmiral is bred to stay further. He has two half-brothers that won over 2m 4f and 2m 5f while his dam is a half-sister to a smart 3m hurdle winner.

Monmiral is a name to note for fences over 2m 4f or more, perhaps sooner rather than later given the trainer's record with young novice chasers. He needs to be slicker over the hurdles to compete with the current crop of Champion Hurdle contenders.

Quilixios ended the season the winner of five of his six starts over hurdles, meeting defeat on his final appearance when beaten 30 lengths by Jeff Kidder in the Grade 1 Champion Four Year Old Hurdle at Punchestown.

Before that he had beaten the consistent Adagio by three and a quarter lengths in the Triumph Hurdle at Cheltenham, having won his previous four starts, first in France and then Punchestown, Down Royal and Leopardstown. He was particularly game at Cheltenham, battling bravely up the hill.

This consistent son of Maxios, bred along Flat-racing lines, does not appeal as an obvious winner of a Champion Hurdle. He has a thoroughly likeable way of going about his racing but connections have suggested that he may switch to chasing, the job for which he was bought.

Metier warrants a mention.

Harry Fry's son of the late Mastercraftsman, a progressive handicapper on the Flat in Ireland, won his first three starts over hurdles for this trainer, at Newton Abbot in October, Ascot in November and then impressively by 12 lengths at Sandown in January.

It was on the strength of that form that he started a well-supported 11/2 for the Supreme Novices' Hurdle but he raced keenly and made a few mistakes, beaten at the second last and finishing 36 lengths behind the winner.

Metier thrives on heavy ground, which could be an issue at Cheltenham in March, but he is the sort of horse who could do well in the pre-Christmas trials, with a consequent reduction in his odds for the Champion Hurdle market.

I can't let this feature pass without a mention of the mercurial **Goshen**.

The wounds from that last-flight fall in the 2020 Triumph Hurdle are still very raw for some, but it seems the horse himself may still be hurting having run two stinkers at the track last season.

On the one occasion he had heavy ground he won, taking the Kingwell Hurdle at Wincanton by 22 lengths from Song For Someone.

At Cheltenham in March he was reluctant to go into the paddock and then hung right through the race, becoming virtually unsteerable.

His trainer Gary Moore says he will be kept to right-handed tracks from now on, with a race at Ascot in November on the agenda. Don't be surprised to see him return to winning ways, although a return to Cheltenham seems most unlikely.

Keep an eye on **Copperless**.

Olly Murphy's son of Kayf Tara gained compensation for his second-last flight fall at Aintree in April when hacking up a month later from a mark of 126 in the Swinton Hurdle at Haydock.

Raised 15lb for that, to 141, he must have a leading chance

in the Greatwood Hurdle at Cheltenham. A successful pre-Christmas campaign could attract speculative interest in the Champion Hurdle market.

A horse that caught most of us on the hop was **Jeff Kidder**.

A high-60s performer on the Flat in 2020, he was beaten in his first two hurdles at Roscommon in August and Punchestown in September, before winning a maiden event at Fairyhouse in November. He then ran last in a Grade 2 contest at Leopardstown and went to Cheltenham from a mark of 125 for the highly competitive Boodles Juvenile Handicap Hurdle, for which he started at 80/1.

Despite a few sloppy jumps and looking held two hurdles from home, he rallied to get back into contention on the run-in to win by two lengths from the well-fancied Saint Sam. This was a gritty affair, with the winner having to come between tiring horses approaching the last.

He then stepped up from that to win a Grade 2 at Fairyhouse before improving again to beat Zanahiyr, who had beaten him by almost nine lengths on Boxing Day, in the Grade 1 Champion Four Year Old Hurdle at Punchestown. Once again he showed impressive battling qualities to hold the determined late challenge of the runner up.

I would not underestimate Jeff Kidder.

He lacks the classy profile and charisma of other Champion Hurdle contenders, but he has successfully tackled the Cheltenham hill and he improved by an official margin of 22lb between the Festival and the end of his campaign.

Trainer Noel Meade has tried him twice on the Flat this summer, from a mark in the low 60s, without success, but on good ground and with chasing not an option, according to the trainer, he has no alternative but to follow the Champion Hurdle route.

He lacks the brilliance of the favourite but his tenacity will stand him in good stead and he appeals as the sort of horse who could become a Festival regular. There is much to like about him.

Conclusion

Honeysuckle is a thoroughly worthy favourite who will, if all goes well, be very hard to beat. She has a flawless record and is blessed with the courage to match her talent. Regarding an ante-post involvement I would have more concern about her sustaining an injury or a mishap of some kind than the opposition.

Bob Olinger, Appreciate It and Ferny Hollow may have their attention switched to chasing. This could leave Epatante and Jeff Kidder, available at 16/1 and 25/1 respectively, as sensible alternatives. The consistent Sharjah, at 20/1, falls into a similar category.

Of the others we need to keep an eye on the progressive Echoes In Rain, who was starting to look quite special in the spring.

The Gold Cup Preview 2022
Marten Julian

The most impressive feature of the 2021 Gold Cup was not something that is likely to have much of a bearing on this season's running.

The highlight was, for me, the breathtaking round of jumping put up by **Frodon**, who took lengths off his rivals at the majority of the fences.

He was virtually flawless, particularly so at the open ditches, relishing his role at the head of affairs in the hands of his regular partner Bryony Frost. He was still there until the final turn, where he was joined by Minella Indo before dropping away to finish fifth, beaten just over 33 lengths at the line.

Frodon – an admirable racehorse in every way

His performance was no surprise. He has always been a most impressive jumper, since his first novice chase win at Newton Abbot back in September 2016, and is now the winner of 15 of his 32 chases, on 23 occasions in the frame.

It was typical of the horse that just over a month after the Gold Cup he battled on gamely to beat Mister Fisher by a neck in the Grade 2 Oaksey Chase at Sandown over an extended 2m 6f.

Frodon has run nine times over three miles or more, on three occasions at Cheltenham, winning there around the 3m 1f of the old course in October 2020 and also around the extended 3m 1f of the new course in January 2019.

It does, though, seem that the extended 3m 2f of the Gold Cup trip is, at that exalted level, beyond him and the intention this season is likely to be a crack at following up last season's victory in the King George VI Chase, when he made all to beat Waiting Patiently and Clan Des Obeaux.

However, plans can change and given Paul Nicholls's competitive approach to the game it is not beyond the realms of possibility that if the ground is good they may have another try for the Gold Cup.

Frodon and Bryony Frost encapsulate everything that there is to love about jump racing and this admirable racehorse, who is still only nine, has more big prizes awaiting him.

The Gold Cup was won in workmanlike style by **Minella Indo**, who was up with the pace throughout and stayed on in gutsy fashion to hold the persistent challenge of stable companion A Plus Tard.

This came on the back of two undistinguished efforts, when falling at halfway in the Savills Chase at Leopardstown over Christmas and then when fourth to Kemboy at the same track in February.

It's possible that the sharp track at Leopardstown probably doesn't play to his strengths.

The previous season he had shown that Cheltenham suits him when just failing to hold the spirited challenge of Champ in the RSA Insurance Novices' Chase. He was especially impressive at the open ditches with his one error coming at the final fence. Despite that, he was just getting the better of Allaho only to get caught close home by the late surge of the winner.

This season everything went well on his first two starts at Wexford and Navan, up with the pace both times and pulling clear to win comfortably at the line.

He had the first fall of his career next time in the Savills Chase at Leopardstown before running a disappointing race in the Irish Gold Cup, finding less than expected after the last to fade back to fourth.

Having also won the 2019 Albert Bartlett over hurdles there is no doubting that Minella Indo likes this place, and that counts for a lot at the Festival.

Minella Indo is a thoroughly genuine old-fashioned sort of chaser, but in what may prove a better class of race he could be found wanting.

My selection for the race in the *Bulletin Book* was **Champ** but he didn't want to know at any stage of the race, making mistakes at the first, third, fifth and sixth before being pulled up before the next.

Champ – let's hope his problems are behind him

He looked totally out of sorts from flag fall and it later transpired that he had a back problem which, trainer Nicky Henderson says, has subsequently had "considerable surgery". Apparently it was an old problem that had been triggered in the Game Spirit Chase at Newbury, something that with hindsight vet Ger Kelly had been worried about beforehand.

The trainer says, "I think at Newbury Champ's exuberance probably created the problem and jarred him, and at Cheltenham he couldn't get off the ground."

The son of King's Theatre has come a long way since his younger days, starting with a debut success at Southwell in January 2017, and a maiden hurdle success three starts later over Court Dreaming, who runs in the colours of my racing club, at Perth in May 2018.

He won five of his seven starts over hurdles, finding City Island two lengths too good for him in the 2019 Ballymore Novices' Hurdle, but has subsequently attained a higher level of form over fences, winning each of his completed starts in the 2019/20 season culminating in an extraordinary success in the RSA Novices' Chase at Cheltenham, where he made up the best part of 10 lengths from the last to beat Minella Indo and Allaho, pulling away at the line.

Champ was keen to get on with things at Cheltenham, but Barry Geraghty did a good job settling him despite his mount's rather ponderous technique over the fences. In fact the only fence where he made headway was the fourth last, in a display of jumping that was consistent with his first three runs. It says much for his class that he was able to produce such a strong surge at the finish after such a clumsy display of fencing.

We saw a much more assured performer on his belated return to action in February.

Intriguingly asked to drop to an extended two miles – a trip that he had never covered either over hurdles or fences – he ran in the Grade 2 Game Spirit Chase and, in finishing two lengths behind the specialist two-miler Sceau Royal, exceeded expectations.

Striding along at the head of affairs he jumped with a hitherto unseen confidence, looking keen to go faster down the back straight. Still leading on the turn for home, he put in his best jump of the race at the third from home and only gave way to the winner approaching the last.

At no stage did his rider resort to the whip as he went down by two lengths, conceding the winner 3lb.

Champ went to Cheltenham a fresh horse, on the back of an excellent run and with course experience to call upon, so it was disappointing that he wasn't right on the day.

As for his stamina his dam is a half-sister to triple Gold Cup winner Best Mate and long-distance winners Cornish Rebel and Inca Trail and the way he finished in the RSA should put any concerns on that score to rest.

With respect to the future there must be a concern that his back problem may reoccur. Connections may try to mitigate this by giving the horse a light campaign, perhaps just one race before Cheltenham, but he will be 10 next spring and time is not on his side.

I believe that Champ has the ability to win a Gold Cup but there are risks attached and he is not an ante-post proposition. He could, though, become of interest nearer the time, as the talent is there.

Al Boum Photo, the winner in 2019 and 2020, was not disgraced in finishing a very creditable third the following year, just over five lengths behind the winner. Turning for home he looked a serious threat, travelling well, but he was kept in for a few strides by A Plus Tard and the front two got away from him approaching the last.

Al Boum Photo – can he win a third Gold Cup?

To his great credit he galloped all the way to the line, not losing any further ground, but trainer Willie Mullins said afterwards that in his view the horse "didn't jump as fluently as last year".

He was certainly deliberate over many of the fences, but he travelled well through the race about five lengths off the pace on ground that may have been a little on the quick side for him.

His season ended with a very gutsy effort to chase home Clan Des Obeaux in the Punchestown Gold Cup, where his chance was compromised by awkward jumps at the third and second last.

The eight-year-old, a son of Buck's Boum – a full brother to Big Buck's – has not caught the public imagination in the way that past dual Gold Cup winners have. Perhaps that is down to the fact that we have seen so little of him. He ran only once before his 2020 victory and just twice prior to his 2019 triumph.

Willie Mullins stuck with his tried and tested formula again last season, with the horse appearing at Tramore on New Year's Day where he beat stable companion Acapella Bourgeois by 19 lengths.

Al Boum Photo enjoyed a relatively smooth passage through the field when winning the race for the first time in 2019, holding the strong-finishing Anibale Fly by two and a half lengths. His jumping had been, for the most part, safe and assured without being spectacular.

The following year his one serious mistake came at the 13th but it didn't cost him any momentum. Taking the lead four fences from home, he was joined by Santini before putting in his best jump at the last, thereby securing an advantage of more than the neck by which he won.

Afterwards Paul Townend said the horse "missed a few fences" but there was no doubting his tenacity from the last.

Al Boum Photo will be 10 next year but he has run just 19 times in his career and will probably follow the same route to Cheltenham as before, with just the one appearance at Tramore in the new year.

It is hard to discount the chance of a horse that has won the Gold Cup twice and finished an honourable third. If he turns out again his record would command the greatest respect.

The runner-up **A Plus Tard** has youth on his side.

Henry De Bromhead's seven-year-old has proved exceptionally consistent throughout his career, never finishing out of the first three in 16 starts, on all but three occasions in the first two.

He had twice run at the Festival leading into last season's race, powering clear to win the 2019 Close Brothers Novices' Handicap Chase by 16 lengths from a mark of 144, and then the following year sticking on well to finish third to Min in the Ryanair over an extended 2m 4f.

Third to Delta Work in a Grade 1 at Punchestown in April 2019, on his only previous start at three miles, he returned to the trip at Leopardstown in the Grade 1 Savills Chase.

Equipped with a tongue-tie for the first time, he travelled well until the home turn, when he came under pressure and looked held. He still seemed to be destined for third after jumping the last until a late and unexpected surge saw him power home and pip Kemboy near the line.

He was held up off the pace in the Gold Cup, lobbing along and generally jumping efficiently though occasionally a little to the right. Clumsy at the seventh from home, losing some momentum, he moved up to within three lengths of the leaders travelling as well as any of his rivals.

Turning for home he was poised to challenge but again he lugged right over the last and despite making relentless progress on the run-in the winner was always holding him on the run to the line.

This was A Plus Tard's first attempt at the trip but there was never much doubt from his pedigree and style of racing that he would get home. It would help his cause if his tendency to jump right could be corrected.

The surprise contender in last year's race was **Royale Pagaille**.

Royale Pagaille – will come into his own when the mud is flying

A fair performer in France, despite winning just once from 10 starts, he ran twice without distinction for Venetia Williams in 2019/20, beaten in a match by Vision Des Flos and then last of three behind Equus Secretus at Huntingdon.

He started last campaign racing from a mark of 135 – over two stones adrift of a Gold Cup rating – but victories off 135, 140 and then by 16 lengths off 156 at Haydock saw his mark rise to 166, leaving him within a few pounds of the leading contenders.

He was most impressive to the eye at Haydock. Lobbing along comfortably within himself, he was always in control and strode away up the straight to win without coming off the bridle.

After much deliberation it was decided to tackle the Gold Cup rather than the National Hunt Chase. It was a brave shout, given that he had been beaten in his first eight starts over fences and that no novice had won the race since Captain Christy in 1974.

In the Gold Cup he was always in arrears – he got close to the third and was on and off the bridle thereafter. Never looking happy in himself, he was able to tag on to the coat-tails of the field for another circuit until switched wide by his rider down the far side for the second time. Back on the bridle, despite a sequence of ponderous jumps, he somehow came home in sixth. The performance was all the more creditable because he lost two shoes and was found to be lame afterwards.

Trainer Venetia Williams said the horse had sustained an injury to his hind foot which was "very, very painful", adding that as it was a hoof injury rather than a bone problem he would "be fine".

There were valid excuses for Royale Pagaille's performance at Cheltenham – the loss of two shoes, the injury and, perhaps as significant, the ground, which was faster than the heavy conditions in which he had been so impressive at Haydock.

With a clean bill of health and on testing ground – unlikely these days at Cheltenham, I concede – Royale Pagaille would have a very good chance of being competitive. Looking back that was not a bad effort last March, given the perfectly valid mitigating circumstances, and he is still a young horse.

Allaho has come up against Minella Indo a few times, beating him on his hurdling debut in February 2019 and then twice finishing behind him at Cheltenham and Punchestown before running a place behind him when third to Champ in the 2020 RSA.

Last season two defeats at Punchestown and Leopardstown were followed by a three-length victory in a 2m 4f Grade 2 at Thurles. It wasn't a convincing display – he made mistakes at the last two fences – but he put up a much better exhibition in the Ryanair Chase, equipped with a tongue-tie for the first time.

Ridden confidently by Rachael Blackmore up at the forefront of affairs, he jumped extremely well, gaining momentum at most of the fences and clearly enjoying himself. By the third last he had his rivals in trouble, pulling clear of the field and turning for home about eight lengths clear and winning by 12 lengths from the staying-on Fakir D'oudairies.

It was no surprise that this display, so impressive to the eye, earned Allaho the accolade of becoming the *Racing Post*'s highest-rated winner of the race, ahead of Cue Card and Vautour.

The following month he chased home Chacun Pour Soi in the 2m William Hill Champion Chase at Punchestown, staying on well over a trip short of his best.

Allaho has not been disgraced over three miles – he won over that distance as a novice hurdler – and out of a half-sister to a

French chase winner over 3m 2f he is entitled to stay the trip, but he looked so good over the extended 2m 4f of the Ryanair that connections are sure to have another crack at the race as his main target.

The horse that for a long time headed the market for the Gold Cup in most lists was **Monkfish**, an incredibly tenacious son of Stowaway who was acquired by Rich Ricci for £235,000 after winning a point-to-point at Stowlin in April 2018.

However in late September Willie Mullins announced that the horse would miss the new season after suffering a tendon injury.

I have, though, experienced many occasions when plans can change so I am retaining these comments, if only for observational interest.

Following a runner-up debut effort to Longhouse Poet in a Punchestown bumper in May 2019, he reappeared that November over hurdles with another second before winning a 2m 7f maiden hurdle at Fairyhouse and then an extended 2m 6f novice hurdle by 20 lengths at Thurles in January.

It was his performance next time in the Albert Bartlett Novices' Hurdle that marked him up.

Galloping up with the pace throughout, despite the occasional ponderous jump, he was challenged on all sides approaching the last and momentarily headed, looking destined for third, before digging deep into his reserves to regain the lead in the dying strides.

It was an extraordinary effort at the end of such a gruelling test and so it was no surprise that he was high on many lists of horses to follow for a novice chasing campaign last season.

His backers were rewarded with four victories from five starts, albeit at odds of 1/2 twice, 1/3 and 1/4. However it was not all plain sailing, as initially he did not look the most natural jumper of a fence.

On his debut at Fairyhouse in November he was measured over the obstacles, warming to his task and lengthening clear of stable companion Ontheropes from the last. A month later he stepped up to three miles for the Grade 1 Neville Hotels Novice Chase at Leopardstown. Occasionally jumping right, he needed firm encouragement from his rider Paul Townend to hold the determined challenge of Latest Exhibition, who had run him to a neck the previous March in the Albert Bartlett.

Next time out in a Grade 1 at Leopardstown he beat the runner-up more easily, dropped down to an extended 2m 5f, with a very fluent display of jumping having travelled well throughout. This was his most impressive display to date, and set him up for the Brown Advisory Novices' Chase, for which he started 1/4 favourite.

Not as fluent on this occasion over the fences, he got close to the second and was slightly hesitant at times, but he stood off at the open ditch and brushed through the top of the fence at the crest of the hill and was joined in the lead by The Big Breakaway. Turning for home he came back on the bridle and had the race in safekeeping until the last, where a mistake would have given his 'bridge jumping' backers a few flurries.

Monkfish suffered his first defeat over fences on his final start at Punchestown in April, clouting the third from home and shuffling over the last before being beaten eight lengths by the mare Colreevy, who was having the final race of her career.

Monkfish is rated on 163, 7lb behind dual Gold Cup winner Al Boum Photo and 12lb behind last season's winner Minella Indo. He has the potential to close the gap, and there are plenty of stayers on the distaff side of his pedigree, but he is a galloper rather than a horse with gears, and this could leave him vulnerable.

I am not convinced that he will travel as well through a race outside novice company and against battle-hardened contenders, while there is also a suspicion that he's a tad lazy.

However this is, in his probable absence, of more long-term relevance.

Envoi Allen has to get himself back into full health and fitness. Latest reports are that he has recovered well from minor surgery.

Unbeaten in his first 11 starts, four in bumpers, including the 2019 Champion Bumper at Cheltenham, and then four times over hurdles – including the following year's Ballymore – he won his next three races over fences at Down Royal, Fairyhouse and Punchestown, before falling at the fourth in the Marsh Novices' Chase and then pulling up lame in the aforementioned race won by Colreevy at Punchestown.

The feature of Envoi Allen's races is his turn of foot.

This was evident in his bumper and hurdling career, and it has stood him in good stead over fences, notably when he quickened twice to beat the now 140-rated Fils D'oudairies, conceding him 11lb, in the Killiney Novice Chase at Punchestown.

Obviously we need Envoi Allen's career to get back on track after two non-finishes, but from what I have seen no current Gold Cup contender has the turn of foot to match this seven-year-old. It's possible that he will be kept at trips short of three miles, but his dam was a successful cross-country performer related to winners over three miles and more and he settles well.

We will soon get an inkling of the trainer's intentions, but I would like to think connections are at least considering the big one. Perhaps an early trial over the trip may encourage them.

Envoi Allen – will they go for the Gold Cup?

Chantry House may also try to make the promotion from last season's novice ranks.

Successful in the second of his point-to-points as a four-year-old, having unseated when leading at the third last on his debut in the race won by Monkfish, he made a winning start under Rules when surging clear to win a Warwick bumper in March 2019.

The following December he landed the odds on his hurdling debut at Cheltenham and followed up at Newbury before running third to Shishkin, beaten 11 lengths, in the Supreme Novices' Hurdle. Time has shown that was a top-class renewal, with the winner and runner-up Abacadabras rated on 153, 13lb superior to Chantry House.

Last season his attention was switched to chasing, starting with a defeat of two rivals in a 2m 3f novice contest at Ascot. The round was not free of blemish, but he powered clear between the last two fences to win with ease.

He was beaten next time at Cheltenham, never travelling that well but subsequently found to be suffering from a kissing spine. He returned to winning ways at Wetherby in February, again coming clear from the last, before stepping up in grade for the Marsh Novices' Chase, for which he started at 9/1.

Kept to the outside of the field from the outset he put in some impressive leaps, travelling well in third down the far side before coming off the bridle on the turn for home. He looked in trouble until the last, when he joined stable companion Fusil Raffles before finding the reserves to pull clear and win by three lengths.

His last race of the season came at Aintree, where he was stepped up to 3m 1f for the Mildmay Novices' Chase. Fortune favoured him when Espoir De Romay came down when two lengths clear at the second last, but this did at least establish he could be effective over three miles, raising hopes for a Gold Cup challenge this season.

Chantry House is rated on 162, 1lb behind Monkfish. He has a better finishing kick than that horse but is not, at this stage, as fluent a jumper. Both, however, have winning Grade 1 form and both should stay the Gold Cup trip. They, together with Envoi Allen, are worthy challengers for the chasing crown.

I think we can assume the mighty **Shishkin** will be kept to two miles over fences.

Having said that, his half-brother won a point-to-point and a hunter chase while his dam won three points and is a half-sister to a 3m hurdle winner. He can, though, be keen and connections have no need to ask him to step up in distance with so much to offer over the minimum trip.

We have not seen 2019 RSA Chase winner **Topofthegame** in action since he ran second to Lostintranslation at Aintree that April. Paul Nicholls has the Grand National in mind if he can get him back to full fitness but latest reports are that he will again miss the season.

Espoir De Romay is not rated far behind last season's top novices.

His mark of 160 is a consequence of that good run at Aintree, where he would have gone close but for the mishap two from home. Two earlier victories at Huntingdon and Leicester, the latter off 140 in a handicap, leave him a long way adrift of the best but trainer Kim Bailey has hopes and he knows what is required to compete at the top.

It is not unreasonable to take the view that **Energumene** could become a contender.

The assumption is that the seven-year-old will follow the top two-mile programme but his sire, the late Denham Red, was an influence for stamina and his dam was a cross-country chase winner and is from a family of stayers.

He beat 17 rivals in a point-to-point on his only start between the flags and made all to win easily by 18 lengths, in heavy ground at Gowran Park, on his sole outing over two and a half miles.

Connections may take the view that the staying programme offers less of a challenge than the very competitive two-mile division.

Delta Work, last seen when third to Kemboy in the Irish Gold Cup in February, missed the remainder of the season. He has a fine Festival record, having won the 2018 Pertemps as a hurdler, then running third to Topofthegame and Santini in the 2019 RSA and fifth to Al Boum Photo in the 2020 Gold Cup.

He will be just nine next spring so still has races in him if he can be brought back to full health and fitness.

Willie Mullins has always thought the world of **Asterion Forlonge**.

The seven-year-old won just twice from seven starts over fences, but he came down twice and had excuses on other occasions. He shaped very well when third to Chantry House in the Marsh Novices' Chase and ran his best race of the season on his final start when carrying 11st 10lb to victory by 14 lengths in a 2m 5f novice handicap chase at Punchestown in April.

The key to this horse could be a step up in trip. One of his half-brothers won over 3m 1f and his dam is a daughter of Turgeon, a profound influence for stamina.

Don't be surprised to see this promising seven-year-old lurking in the wings as the season unfolds.

The trainer has high hopes for the less-exposed **Castlebawn West**.

The eight-year-old son of Westerner wasn't seen out again after beating 21 rivals in the 3m Paddy Power Handicap Chase at Leopardstown over Christmas. The plan had been to aim next at the Grand National or the Irish National, and there is a sense of unfinished business about him. He could be one to keep an eye on.

It's not beyond the realms of possibility that **Saint Calvados** could enter the fray.

The eight-year-old is now with Paul Nicholls having won eight times for his previous trainer Harry Whittington. He didn't appear to get home when dropping away in the closing stages of the King George VI Chase, but he travelled very well for a long way and may settle better for the change of yard.

His trainer relishes a challenge and the horse may benefit from having had a breathing operation this summer.

Not much went right for Colin Tizzard's team last season but **The Big Breakaway** was on the cusp of top-class novice chase form, running a particularly good race when third to Monkfish at Cheltenham in March.

He had shaped with great promise as a hurdler, winning impressively at Chepstow and Newbury before finishing fourth to Envoi Allen in the Ballymore Novices' Hurdle at Cheltenham.

At the age of six he has time on his side and I expect him to progress for the switch to staying handicap chases.

Henry De Bromhead may eke out more improvement from the lightly raced **Eklat De Rire**.

The seven-year-old won his sole point-to-point and has won three of his five starts under Rules. He won both his completed starts over fences, on heavy ground at Punchestown in December and Naas in January, where he was ridden prominently to win over the extended 3m 1f. He then unseated his rider when travelling well in third behind Monkfish at Cheltenham.

He stays and loves the mud and, currently rated on 152, he is poised to take a step up in class.

Finally, it's not uncommon for a horse to emerge as a Gold Cup contender from the previous season's handicap ranks, and **Galvin**, unbeaten in five starts last campaign, warrants a mention.

Galvin – a possible Gold Cup outsider

It took him five runs before winning his first chase, at Killarney in July 2020, but he then won his next four starts, back there in August and then a Grade 3 at Tipperary in October and over an extended 3m at Cheltenham. His final run came when he beat Next Destination in the 3m 6f National Hunt Chase, a success that saw his mark rise to 154.

Galvin has two key factors in his favour.

The first is that he is very effective on good ground, which often prevails at the Festival. The second is that he is a proven stayer, having won over almost half a mile further than the Gold Cup trip. It is encouraging to see that there has been market interest in the horse at long odds.

It will be interesting to learn what connections have in mind, but after the last few months trainer Gordon Elliott will be keen to have his name back in the lights for all the right reasons.

Conclusion

Champ, back to full health, has the ability to win a Gold Cup and 20/1 is tempting, but it's hard to recommend him at this stage given the nature of his problem. Chantry House has, like Champ, had a back problem and 14/1 does not appeal at this time.

At 20/1 Al Boum Photo makes more appeal. We know how he will be campaigned and his performance in three Gold Cups stands up to the closest inspection.

There is no reason why Minella Indo and A Plus Tard should not again have parts to play but the one that could represent value as the best outsider at 50/1 is Galvin.

He likes Cheltenham, handles good ground and stays beyond the Gold Cup trip. However, I have not heard whether the Gold Cup is on his agenda.

Royale Pagaille warrants a mention in the unlikely event the ground in March is testing. I believe he can be excused last year's defeat and has more to offer. At 40/1 he is on the cusp of being interesting value.

The one that I am keenest on is Envoi Allen.

Again we have to trust he has recovered from his injury, but he is bred to stay, has a tremendous winning record and is blessed with a formidable turn of foot. Connections have already stated that the Gold Cup will be his target.

Next best are Al Boum Photo and Galvin. Keep Royale Pagaille in mind if you think we're in for a mudbath.

Index

A PLUS TARD	101
ABACADABRAS	81
AL BOUM PHOTO	98
ALLAHO	104
APPRECIATE IT	83
ARTHUR'S SEAT	60
ASPIRE TOWER	49
ASTERION FORLONGE	111
ASTIGAR	34
BASS ROCK	6
BILL BAXTER	62
BOB OLINGER	82
BROOMFIELD BURG	18
CAPE GENTLEMAN	51
CASTLEBAWN WEST	112
CHAMP	95
CHAMP KIELY	35
CHANTRY HOUSE	109
COPPERLESS	90
CROSSED MY MIND	52
CROSSING THE BAR	19
DALAMOI	63
DELTA WORK	111
DHOWIN	37
DOYEN DU BAR	64
DRAGONFRUIT	19

DREAMS OF HOME	38
DUSART	7
ECHOES IN RAIN	53
ECHOES IN RAIN	86
EDWARDSTONE	9
EKLAT DE RIRE	113
EL BARRA	20
ENERGUMENE	111
ENVOI ALLEN	107
EPATANTE	79
ESCARIA TEN	40
ESPOIR DE ROMAY	110
FAKIERA	10
FERNY HOLLOW	85
FIVE O'CLOCK	12
FLAME BEARER	65
FRENCHY DU LARGE	21
FRODON	93
GAILLARD DU MESNIL	54
GARS DE SCEAUX	42
GARS DE SCEAUX	55
GENTLEMAN JOE	56
GERRI COLOMBE	13
GOSHEN	90
GRANGECLARE WEST	22
GUARDINO	66

HARRY ALONZO	57
HILLCREST	22
HILLCREST	67
HOB HOUSE	68
HOLLOW GAMES	14
HONEYSUCKLE	76
HUNTERS YARN	68
JEFF KIDDER	91
JONBON	23
JOURNEY WITH ME	43
JUMPING JET	58
JUMPING JET	69
KILBEG KING	70
KINCARDINE	24
MASACCIO	24
MERCUTIO ROCK	25
METIER	89
MIGHTY POTTER	15
MINELLA INDO	94
MISTER COFFEY	15
MONKFISH	105
MONMIRAL	87
MR GLASS	26
MR INCREDIBLE	58
MULBERRY HILL	27
MURVAGH BEACH	28

O'TOOLE	29
PILOT SHOW	45
QUILIXIOS	89
RED LION LAD	17
REVASSER	71
ROYAL ARCADE	30
ROYALE PAGAILLE	102
SAINT CALVADOS	112
SAINT PATRIC	72
SHALLWEHAVEONEMORE	73
SHARJAH	81
SHISHKIN	110
SOFT RISK	74
STONE MAD	46
SUPREME GIFT	31
THE BIG BREAKAWAY	112
THREE STRIPE LIFE	31
TIMELESS BEAUTY	47
TOPOFTHEGAME	110
VINA ARDANZA	32
ZINC WHITE	33

Notes